CYBER CRIME

- Capital Punishment
- Criminal Terminology
- Cyber Crime
- Daily Prison Life
- Domestic Crime
- Famous Trials
- Forensic Science
- Global Terrorism
- Government Intelligence Agencies
- Hate Crimes
- The History of Punishment
- The History of Torture
- Infamous Prisons
- Organized Crime
- Protecting Yourself Against Criminals
- Race and Crime
- Serial Murders
- Unsolved Crimes
- The U.S. Justice System
- The War on Drugs

CYBER CRIME

Andrew Grant-Adamson

Foreword by Manny Gomez, Esq.

MASON CREST

Mason Crest
450 Parkway Drive, Suite D
Broomall, PA 19008
www.masoncrest.com

Printed and bound in the United States of America

First printing
9 8 7 6 5 4 3 2 1

Series ISBN: 978-1-4222-3469-3
Hardcover ISBN: 978-1-4222-3471-6
ebook ISBN: 978-1-4222-8398-1

Library of Congress Cataloging-in-Publication Data on file with the Library of Congress

Developed and Produced by Print Matters Productions, Inc. (www.printmattersinc.com)

Developmental Editor: Amy Hackney Blackwell
Cover and Interior Design: Tom Carling, Carling Design Inc.

Note on Statistics: While every effort has been made to provide the most up-to-date government statistics, the Department of Justice and other agencies compile new data at varying intervals, sometimes as much as ten years. Agency publications are often based on data compiled from a period ending a year or two before the publication date.

CONTENTS

Foreword by Manny Gomez, Esq. 6

The Community of Cyberspace 11

The Hackers 23

The Threat Inside 37

Business Under Attack 47

Virus Attack 61

Law Enforcement and Security 73

Series Glossary 83

Chronology 90

Further Information 93

Index.. 95

Picture Credits 96

KEY ICONS TO LOOK FOR:

 Text-Dependent Questions: These questions send the reader back to the text for more careful attention to the evidence presented there.

 Words to Understand: These words with their easy-to-understand definitions will increase the reader's understanding of the text while building vocabulary skills.

 Series Glossary of Key Terms: This back-of-the-book glossary contains terminology used throughout this series. Words found here increase the reader's ability to read and comprehend higher-level books and articles in this field.

 Research Projects: Readers are pointed toward areas of further inquiry connected to each chapter. Suggestions are provided for projects that encourage deeper research and analysis.

 Sidebars: This boxed material within the main text allows readers to build knowledge, gain insights, explore possibilities, and broaden their perspectives by weaving together additional information to provide realistic and holistic perspectives.

FOREWORD

Experience Counts

Detecting crime and catching lawbreakers is a very human endeavor. Even the best technology has to be guided by human intelligence to be used effectively. If there's one truth from my thirty years in law enforcement and security, it's trust your gut.

When I started on the police force, I learned from older officers and from experience what things to look for, what traits, characteristics, or indicators lead to somebody who is about to commit a crime or in the process of committing one. You learn from experience. The older generation of law enforcement teaches the younger generation, and then, if you're good, you pick up your own little nuances as to what bad guys are doing.

In my early work, I specialized in human intelligence, getting informants to tell me what was happening on the street. Most of the time it was people I arrested that I then "flipped" to inform me where the narcotics were being stored, how they were being delivered, how they were being sold, the patterns, and other crucial details.

A good investigator has to be organized since evidence must be presented in a legally correct way to hold up in court. Evidence from a crime scene has to have a perfect chain of custody. Any mishandling turns the evidence to fruits of a poisonous tree.

At my company, MG Security Services, which provides private security to corporate and individual clients in the New York area, we are always trying to learn and to pass on that learning to our security officers in the field.

Certainly, the field of detection has evolved dramatically in the last 100 years. Recording devices have been around for a long time; it's just that now they've gotten really good. Today, a pen can be a video recording device; whereas in the old days it would have been a large box with two wheels. The equipment was awkward and not too subtle: it would be eighty degrees out, you'd be sweating in a raincoat, and the box would start clicking.

The forensic part of detection is very high-tech these days, especially with DNA coming into play in the last couple of decades. A hundred years ago, fingerprinting revolutionized detective work; the next breakthrough is facial recognition. We have recently discovered that the arrangement of facial features (measured as nodes) is unique to each individual. No two people on the planet have the exact same configuration of nodes. Just as it took decades to build out the database of known fingerprints, facial recognition is a work in progress. We will see increasing collection of facial data when people obtain official identification. There are privacy concerns, but we're working them out. Facial recognition will be a centerpiece of future detection and prevention efforts.

Technology offers law enforcement important tools that we're learning to apply strategically. Algorithms already exist that allow retailers to signal authorities when someone makes a suspicious purchase—known bomb-making ingredients, for example. Cities are loaded with sensors to detect the slightest trace of nuclear, biological, or chemical materials that pose a threat to the public. And equipment nested on streetlights in New York City can triangulate the exact block where a gun was fired.

Now none of this does anything constructive without well-trained professionals ready and able to put the information to use. The tools evolve, but what doesn't evolve is human intelligence.

Law enforcement as a community is way ahead in fighting street and violent crime than the newer challenges of cybercrime and terrorism. Technology helps, but it all goes back to human intelligence. There is no substitute for the cop on the street, knowing what is going on in the neighborhood, knowing who the players are. When the cop has quality informants inside gangs, he or she knows when there's going to be a hit, a drug drop, or an illicit transaction. The human intelligence comes first; then you can introduce the technology, such as hidden cameras or other surveillance.

The twin challenges for domestic law enforcement are gangs and guns. Gangs are a big problem in this country. That's a cultural and social phenomenon that law enforcement has not yet found an effective way to counteract. We need to study that more diligently. If we're successful in getting rid of the gangs, or at least diluting them, we will have come a long way in fighting violent crime. But guns are the main issue. You look at England, a first-world country of highly educated people that strictly regulates guns, and the murder rate is minimal.

When it comes to cybercrime, we're woefully behind. That's simply because we hire people for the long term, and their skills get old. You have a twenty-five-year-old who's white-hot now, but guess what? In five years that skill set is lost. Hackers, on the other hand, are young people who tend to evolve fast. They learn so much more than their older law-enforcement counterparts and are able to penetrate systems too easily. The Internet was not built with the security of private users in mind. It is like a house with no door locks, and now we're trying to figure ways to secure the house. It was done kind of backward. Nobody really thought that it was going to be this wide-open door to criminal activity.

We need to change the equation for cybercriminals. Right now the chances are they won't get caught; cybercrime offers criminals huge benefit at very little cost. Law enforcement needs to recruit young people who can match skills with the criminals. We also need to work closely with foreign governments and agencies to better identify, deter, and apprehend cybercriminals. We need to make examples of them.

Improving our cybercrime prevention means a lot more talent, a lot more resources, a lot more hands-on collaboration with countries on the outskirts—Russia, China, even Israel. These are the countries that are constantly trying to penetrate our cyberspace. And even if we are able to identify the person overseas, we still need the cooperation of the overseas government and law enforcement to help us find and apprehend the person. Electrical grids are extremely vulnerable to cyber attacks. Utilities built long before the Internet need engineering retrofits to make them better able to withstand attacks.

As with cybercrime, efforts against terrorism must be coordinated to be effective. Communication is crucial among all levels of law enforcement, from local law enforcement and national agencies sharing information—in both directions—to a similar international flow of information among different countries' governments and national bureaus. In the U.S., since 9/11, the FBI and local law enforcement now share a lot more information with each other locally and nationally. Internationally, as well, we are sharing more information with Interpol and other intelligence and law enforcement agencies throughout the world to be able to better detect, identify, and prevent criminal activity

When it comes to terrorism, we also need to ramp up our public relations. Preventing terror attacks takes more than a military response. We need to address this culture of death with our own Internet media campaign and 800 numbers to make it easy for people to reach out to law enforcement and help build the critical human infrastructure. Without people, there are no leads—people on the inside of a criminal enterprise are essential to directing law enforcement resources effectively, telling you when to listen, where to watch, and which accounts to check.

In New York City, the populace is well aware of the "see something, say something" campaign. Still, we need to do more. More people need to speak up. Again, it comes down to trusting your instincts. If someone seems a little off to you, find a law enforcement representative and share your perception. Listen to your gut. Your gut will always tell you: there's something hinky going on here. Human beings have a sixth sense that goes back to our caveman days when animals used to hunt us. So take action, talk to law enforcement when something about a person makes you uneasy or you feel something around you isn't right.

We have to be prepared not just on the prevention side but in terms of responses. Almost every workplace conducts a fire drill at least once a year. We need to do the same with active-shooter drills. Property managers today may even have their own highly trained active-shooter teams, ready to be on site within minutes of any attack.

We will never stop crime, but we can contain the harm it causes. The coordinated efforts of law enforcement, an alert and well-trained citizenry, and the smart use of DNA, facial profiles, and fingerprinting will go a long way toward reducing the number and severity of terror events.

Be it the prevention of street crime or cybercrime, gang violence or terrorism, sharing information is essential. Only then can we put our technology to good use. People are key to detection and prevention. Without the human element, I like to say a camera's going to take a pretty picture of somebody committing a crime.

Law enforcement must strive to attract qualified people with the right instincts, team-sensibility, and work ethic. At the end of the day, there's no hunting like the hunting of man. It's a thrill; it's a rush; and that to me is law enforcement in its purest form.

MANNY GOMEZ, Esq.

President of MG Security Services,

Chairman of the National Law Enforcement Association,

former FBI Special Agent,

U.S. Marine, and NYPD Sergeant

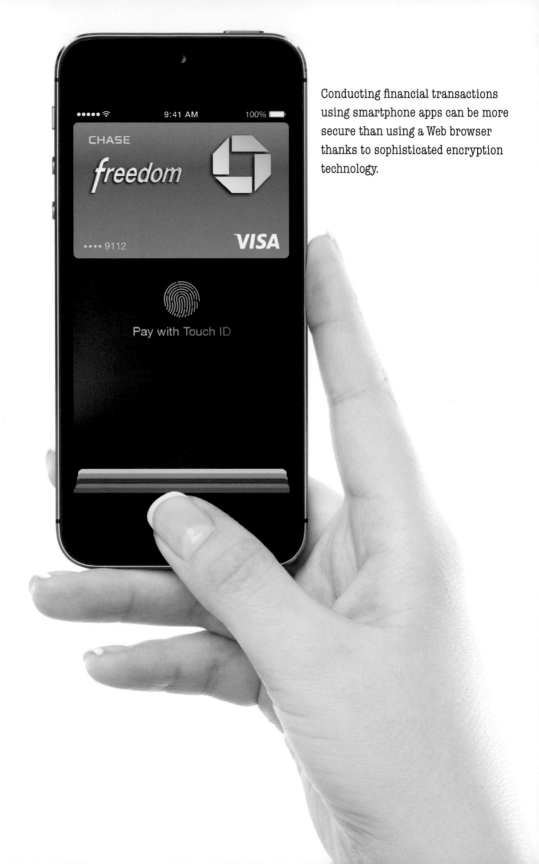

Conducting financial transactions using smartphone apps can be more secure than using a Web browser thanks to sophisticated encryption technology.

CYBER
CRIME

CHAPTER 1

THE COMMUNITY OF CYBERSPACE

Words to Understand

Cyber crime: crime involving the use of networked computers

Disgruntled: discontented

Hacker: someone who is a computer expert or someone who gains illegal access to computer systems

Internet Service Provider (ISP): business that provides customers with access to the Internet

Jurisprudence: a system or body of law

Xenophobic: having an unreasonable fear of what is foreign and especially of people of foreign origin

CYBERSPACE IS A NEW TERRITORY, A NEW DIMENSION ALMOST, IN WHICH WE LIVE AND WORK. FOR EXAMPLE, I HAVE A QUESTION FOR A COLLEAGUE WHO WORKS IN AN OFFICE TWO DOORS DOWN THE HALL. ONCE, I WOULD HAVE PICKED UP THE TELEPHONE, BUT NOW I USE E-MAIL. THE REPLY COMES BACK MINUTES LATER. IT TURNS OUT HE IS NOT IN HIS OFFICE, BUT IN AUSTRALIA. I HAD NOT REALIZED THAT, BUT IT DOES NOT MATTER—WE CAN DO OUR BUSINESS JUST AS EASILY 12 YARDS OR 12,000 MILES APART. HOWEVER, ALONG WITH THE BENEFITS OF NEW TERRITORY COMES NEW CRIME.

Never before has a new technology been taken up faster than the Internet. Growth, driven by the World Wide Web, started to explode in the last decade of the 20th century, linking people in ways never contemplated (and never possible) before. The benefits are immense, but criminals have found opportunities too.

What Is Cyber Crime?

Cyber crime is any type of crime performed over computer networks. As more and more of our lives take place online, more and more criminal operations migrate there as well. In the 2010s, cyber crime has cost the global economy billions of dollars yearly.

New types of cyber crime appear constantly. They include financial crimes, such as credit card theft and fraud; identity theft; attacks on networks to steal information; and abuse, particularly sex crimes, prostitution, and sexual exploitation of children. The world's law enforcement agencies have jumped into the fray and are trying to stay ahead of the criminals—or at least not too far behind them.

Opening Up New Territories

Not long after Christopher Columbus voyaged from Spain to the Americas, fortune hunters and pirates roamed the oceans to steal the gold that had been found there. Entrepreneurs persuaded the optimistic, or the gullible, to invest in new ventures that were doomed to fail. Investors in England poured money into a company that promised huge profits from trade with South America. The South Sea Bubble and the collapse of that business in the early 1700s, remains one of the most notorious corporate failures in history. In the new millennium, dot-com collapses echoed that disaster.

Opening up the American West in the 19th century brought robbers, gambling, share swindles, and cattle rustling in its wake. Western movies celebrate the battles between good guys and bad guys. Without new technology, the West would not have been won so quickly: the railroad and telegraph made the rapid exploitation of a huge new territory possible. Nor would it have been won so quickly without the mavericks, those that rejected authority and cut corners. A fine line divides heroes and villains.

Cyberspace is also a new territory. As in the past, it is criminals who have been among the first to recognize the potential of a wide-open, sparsely populated, and poorly policed space. The crimes are similar, too. Theft, fraud, breaking and entering, vandalism, illegal betting, the sex trade, and investment scams are all a part of the Internet crime wave. Law enforcement agencies are fighting to keep up with an explosion of crimes that do not recognize international boundaries.

Promises of riches have always attracted investors. In London in the early 18th century, the South Sea Company collapsed, and the downfall of that business is remembered even today when we talk about the "bubble" bursting to describe dot-com failures.

Big sporting events, like the soccer World Cup, give a massive boost to betting organizations around the globe. Legal betting shops, like this one in Macao, face increasing competition from offshore Internet gambling, which can escape national laws and regulation, and is sometimes open to fraud and money laundering as funds move rapidly through cyberspace.

International Cooperation

Police around the world have had to reinvent themselves as they battle against new kinds of criminals. They are up against something entirely new. The following is a true example. A Visa card was used by a man (myself) in an English village to buy software from a company in California. A **hacker** in an unknown location found the number of the credit card and sold it to another criminal in the United States. It was then used to place bets totaling $6,000 with a betting Web site in Costa Rica. The Web site used a credit card merchant service in Montreal, Canada, to process its transactions. The Canadian business banked in Port of Spain, Trinidad. The Caribbean bank debited the card-issuing bank in Manchester, England. The computer at that bank was bright enough to recognize that I did not have a history of gambling and raised the alarm. Police in at least five countries could have an interest in the case, but how can they gather evidence? And where exactly was the crime committed?

Anyone given a blank piece of paper and asked to provide a solution to the policing of cyberspace would quickly come up with an answer: an international police force. However, such a force is not on the political agenda anywhere. The traditions of **jurisprudence** are too varied. Even countries that are apparently cooperating well and that have similar traditions experience difficulties.

For example, Europe does not have the same near-absolute attachment to freedom of speech as the United States, where it is embodied in the Constitution through the Fourth Amendment. This became an issue when France wanted to ban access to Internet auctions of Nazi memorabilia. In Europe, there have been concerns about the possibility of providing evidence from computers that might help convict a terrorist in the United States, where he could face the death penalty. Most European countries will not assist in any trial that might end with capital punishment. Britain, for example, insists on a guarantee that the court will not impose a death sentence.

The Rise of the Internet Community

By 2014, it was estimated that 38 percent of the world's population had used the Internet that year. In the developed world, Internet connections are ubiquitous, and many people carry or wear devices that are online at all times. Internet-connected computers are now small enough to wear as watches or in the frames of eyeglasses.

But the Internet is really a very new phenomenon. Teenagers of the 2010s cannot remember when it did not exist; their parents remember those days very well.

Numbers online worldwide in the Internet's early days:

Year	Number	% population
2002	544.2 m	8.96
2001	455.55 m	7.55
2000	280.86 m	4.63
1999	153.5 m	3.75
1998	119 m	2.91
1997	74 m	1.81
1996	55 m	1.31
1995	26 m	0.63

While the Internet has its roots in a network developed for the military and research institutions in the 1960s, it first became available to the public in the 1970s. The breakthrough was the development of the World Wide Web by Tim Berners-Lee at Cern, the European particle physics lab, in 1989. Internet traffic increased 25-fold between then and 1994. Then the most rapid rise in access to a new technology in world history started.

An International Success Story

Where there is agreement, law enforcement agencies are beginning to cooperate effectively. At the end of summer 2001, police in 12 countries carried out simultaneous raids to seize computers and arrest more than 200 people. Bob Packham, deputy director general of the British National Crime Squad, which coordinated the operation, said, "I am unaware of no other police operation that has pulled together so many law enforcement agencies worldwide to effect simultaneous raids and arrests." The police claimed that they had broken the largest and most sophisticated pedophile group on the Internet. Indeed, more than a million images of children were found.

The story started five years earlier when a pornographic network in San Francisco revealed links to England. British police uncovered the Wonderland Club, whose members had to "pay" a joining fee of thousands of pictures. In the United States, 34 people were arrested in 31 cities.

Doris Gardner, former chief of the FBI Computer Crimes Unit in Charlotte, North Carolina, one of the only eight such special units in the United States. A half dozen agents work in the office that opened in 2014.

Former FBI Director Louis J. Freeh struggled to combat a massive increase in cyber crime following the development of the World Wide Web. He admitted the agency faced serious problems because of the rapid increase in computer crime.

U.S. Customs Commissioner Raymond Kelly said that anyone who thought they could hide behind a maze of **Internet Service Providers** (ISPs), servers, files, and screen names was wrong. "We will find them and bring them to justice," he said.

In 2001 the European Union, the United States, Canada, and Japan created an international treaty, the Convention on Cyber Crime, that sought to bring the laws in these countries much more closely into line and empower police to investigate on behalf of law enforcers in member countries. By 2015, 46 nations had ratified the convention. Russia opposed it and refused to cooperate with law enforcement investigations of cyber crime that involved Russian suspects. The convention covers data interference, forgery and fraud, child pornography, and copyright and usage right infringements.

Categorizing Cyber Crime

The main categories of cyber crime have been in place since the start of the 2000s.

- Insider threat—The **disgruntled** insider is a principal source of computer crime. More than half the businesses and organizations responding to a survey reported malicious activity by employees or those who had been employees until shortly before the attack.
- Hackers—Sometimes hackers crack networks simply for the thrill of the challenge and to brag about it. Recently, there has been a rise in cases of hacking for illicit financial gain or other malicious purposes.
- Hacktivism—Politically motivated attacks are placed on publicly accessible Web pages and e-mail servers to send a political message.
- Virus writers—Viruses pose an increasingly serious threat to networks and systems worldwide.
- Criminal groups—The FBI is seeing the increased use of cyber-intrusions by criminal groups who attack systems for monetary gain.
- Distributed denial of service attacks (DDOS attacks)—These are attacks that flood Internet servers with information that requires a response, thus causing servers to crash or slow traffic to a crawl.
- Terrorists—Terrorists are known to use information technology and the Internet to formulate plans, raise funds, spread propaganda, and communicate securely. Pornography and other forms of sexual exploitation are also common on the Internet. Sexual predators use social media to stalk their victims, and child pornography is a well-known problem.
- Sensitive intrusions—In recent years, there has been a series of intrusions into Department of Defense computer networks, as well as those of other federal agencies, universities, and private-sector entities. Enormous amounts of material have been taken.
- Information warfare—Nations can use computers as a tool for espionage waging war.

Sexual exploitation, terrorism, and the hacking of government documents are large crimes, but cyber crime affects individuals as well, and at all income levels. By 2015 it was typical for banks to issue new credit cards on a regular basis simply because data was so often hacked. The Internet Crime Complaint Center reported that the following categories of cyber crime were common in the 2010s:

- Auction fraud: including non-delivery of goods, fraud involving payment, and counterfeit goods.

- Counterfeit cashier's checks: a person outside the U.S. contacts someone and asks him or her to receive a large sum of money in the form of a certified bank check, returning a portion of that money through a wire transfer. The check turns out to be fraudulent but the transfer of cash is real.
- Credit card fraud.
- Debt elimination, websites selling methods of disposing of mortgages for a fee. This crime also involves identity theft.
- Parcel courier email scheme.
- Fake employment or business opportunities.
- Escrow services fraud.
- Identity theft: a thief uses another person's personal information to commit crimes.
- Internet extortion.
- Investment fraud.
- Fake lotteries.
- Phishing and spoofing, involving forged electronic documents or fake emails used to get people to divulge personal information that can be used for identity theft or credit card fraud.
- Ponzi and pyramid schemes.
- Spam.

Raphael Gray hacked into Internet shopping sites around the world and stole the credit card details of 23,000 people. The FBI said his activities could have cost $3 million. The judge who sentenced Gray to three years community rehabilitation with psychiatric care said he had shown a "sense of humor" by using a stolen credit card number to send Viagra tablets to Microsoft boss Bill Gates.

Cyber Crime Convention

In the fall of 2001, 31 nations signed the Cyber Crime Convention, drawn up by the Council of Europe. Forty-six nations had ratified it as of 2015. The Convention covers three main topics: harmonization of national laws, prosecution procedures to cope with global networks, and rapid and effective international cooperation. There are four main categories of offenses:

1. Offenses against the confidentiality, integrity, and availability of computer data and systems.

2. Computer-related offenses, such as forgery and computer fraud.

3. Content-related offenses, such as the production, dissemination, and posses-sion of child pornography; a section on the propagation of racist and **xeno-phobic** ideas was to be added.

4. Offenses related to infringement of copyright and related rights; the wide-scale distribution of pirated copies of protected works, and so on.

New Procedures

The Convention embodies basic rules that will make it easier for police to investigate computer crimes. To protect human rights, these rules are subject to conditions and safeguards in the laws of member states.

International Cooperation

Police in one country will be able to collect computer-based evidence for police in another, although they will not be able to conduct investigations or searches across borders. Information obtained must be passed on rapidly for quick response.

The fight against cyber crime has moved to the heart of government. The Department of Homeland Security and the National Security Council, whose White House situation room is pictured here, has taken a leading role in the battle, and one of its top officials, Michael Daniel, was chosen by President Obama as his special adviser on cyber security.

Text-Dependent Questions

1. What is the Internet?
2. What are some of the more common types of cyber crime?
3. What is the Cyber Crime Convention?

Research Projects

1. What cyber crimes is the FBI pursuing right now?
2. How can you protect yourself and your devices from cyber crime?
3. How do terrorists use the Internet to facilitate their activities?

THE HACKERS

Words to Understand

Password: a data string used to verify the identity of a user
Phreaker: a person who hacks telephone systems
Restitution: a making good of or giving an equivalent for some injury

EARLY HACKERS WERE HEROES. THEY WERE THE PEOPLE WHO MADE THE COMPUTER REVOLUTION HAPPEN. THEY WORKED IN PLACES LIKE THE MASSACHUSETTS INSTITUTE OF TECHNOLOGY ARTIFICIAL INTELLIGENCE LAB. THIS WAS ONE OF THE PLACES LINKED TO THE ARPANET, THE FORERUNNER OF THE INTERNET, SHORTLY AFTER ITS FOUNDATION IN 1969. XEROX'S FAMED PALO ALTO RESEARCH CENTER WAS ANOTHER LAB WHERE HACKERS WORKED. PALO ALTO WAS A POWERHOUSE OF IDEAS THAT INFLUENCED THE WAY COMPUTERS WERE TO BE USED. THE MOUSE, ICONS, AND WINDOWS—THE GRAPHIC USER INTERFACE (GUI)—ALL CAME FROM THERE.

What are Hackers?

A hacker is a person who attempts to enter supposedly secure computer networks. Most important networks are protected with **passwords** and limited access; this is necessary to protect confidential and valuable information. But no security system is perfect, and hackers specialize in finding weaknesses in network security. A hacker might engage in hacking as a hobby; or he might want to enter systems to steal data, get access to money, find personal information he can use to blackmail someone, or some other evil purpose.

Ping... the complex route a message has taken from the other side of the world on the information superhighway flashes up on the screen. Most users just want their computer to work. But others want to know how it works; they are the hackers. Increasingly, they are also criminals.

Hackers–Real and Imaginary

Seymour Cray, designer of the supercomputers that carried his name, was a hacker. His machines transformed weather forecasting and were widely used by governments for breaking codes and analysis.

Dennis Ritchie and Ken Thompson of the Bell Labs' computer science group created Unix, the operating system for minicomputers. Unix servers continue to provide much of the backbone of the Web. Richard Stallman got a job at MIT's artificial intelligence lab while he was still an undergraduate at Harvard. He did not believe software should be private property and founded the Free Software Foundation. These men were typical of the early hackers. They could make computers do things that others could not imagine and were driving the revolution.

In 1984, the film *War Games* brought into question the relationship between people, computers, and decisions about nuclear war. Here, the hero David Lightman, played by Matthew Broderick, works at the home computer he uses to hack the National Defense System.

Then, in 1984, came the movie *War Games*, in which teenager David Lightman (played by Matthew Broderick) hacks into a computer and starts playing Global Thermonuclear War. To him, this is just a game, but the computer, War Operational Research, is interested in more serious games. It is a part of the U.S. National Defense System, and David is actually playing with a simulation of nuclear war. He triggers a national emergency that raises questions about the relationship of humans and computers. The futuristic sets added to the glamor of what David found himself doing. *War Games* was credited with igniting the interest of teenage boys in hacking back in the 1980s. They found breaking into computers a challenge, and some went beyond that, causing real damage.

So, What Is Hacking?

Webster's Collegiate Dictionary gives two computer-related meanings to the word "hacker." The first is "an expert at programing and solving problems with a computer." The second is "a person who illegally gains access to and sometimes tampers with information in a computer system." The second meaning has come to dominate, although old-style hackers are resentful at the misuse of the word.

Hacking costs businesses, government agencies, and other organizations worldwide huge sums of money. How much is impossible to judge because many incidents go unreported. The Center for Strategic and International Studies estimated that cyber crime cost the global economy some $115 billion in 2012, $160 billion of that losses to individuals and the rest losses to businesses. Within the United States about 40 million people had had information stolen by hackers.

Secrets of the Little Blue Box

In 1971, the world reveled in the story of John Draper, who chose the pseudonym "Cap'n Crunch" to hide his identity. He found a toy whistle in a packet of the breakfast cereal and realized it produced the 2600-hertz tone needed to access phone lines. He made a little blue box to generate the dialing tones to make free long-distance calls.

Esquire magazine brought him fame with an article entitled, "Secrets of the Little Blue Box." If it was not for that publicity, he might never have gone to jail. The article led to an international following, including college kids Steve Wozniak and Steve Jobs, who went on to found Apple Computers. Free calls lasted until phone companies updated their systems. *Newsweek* many years later put Cap'n Crunch in their top-20 list of hackers.

The FBI sees hacking as an increasingly serious crime. As the Internet has expanded, so have the opportunities for hacking—more people with computers at home means more targets. Criminals who are out to steal money, secrets, and the identities of other people have overtaken teenagers as the main threat in the eyes of law enforcement agencies. Identity theft—pretending to be someone else by stealing their personal information, such as name, date of birth, social security number (SSN), and credit card details—has been called the crime of the new millennium. Identity thieves use old-fashioned methods like dumpster-diving and street robbery, as well as hacking computer databases for information.

The First Federal Computer Case Against a Juvenile

Against this background, police around the world have lost patience with teenage hackers. At 9:00 A.M. on March 10, 1997, phones were cut off at Worcester Airport in Massachusetts. The control tower and the fire department were cut off. The main radio at the tower would not work. After six-and-a-half hours, the system started operating again. At almost the same time as airport communications were restored, the whole phone system in Rutland, Massachusetts, went down. U.S. Secret Service Acting Special Agent in Charge Michael T. Johnston said, "This case, with the associated national security ramifications, is one of the most significant computer-fraud investigations conducted by the U.S. Secret Service."

The attack showed the vulnerability of thousands of similar telephone-company computers across the country. These loop-carrier systems integrate voice and data coming down copper phone lines for transmission over a sophisticated fiber-optic cable. "Just as disabling a circuit breaker box blacks out an entire house, so disabling a loop-carrier system cut off all communications with the telephone lines it services," explained U.S. Attorney Donald K. Stern.

One of thousands of computer hackers at the Beyond HOPE (Hackers on Planet Earth) convention in New York. Many hackers see themselves as "white hats" that expose the failures of computer companies to make their products secure. "Black hats" are the criminal hackers, but the distinction is less and less recognized by the law.

The hacker was a teenage boy who, under federal law, cannot be named. It was the first computer crime case brought against a juvenile under federal law. Attorney Stern said:

> Computer and telephone networks are at the heart of vital services provided by the government and private industry, and are critical infrastructure. They are not toys for the entertainment of teenagers. Hacking a computer or telephone network can create a tremendous risk to the public.... This case reflects our intention to prosecute in a federal court anyone, including a teenager, who commits a serious computer crime.

The teenager was put on probation and banned from remotely accessing a computer for two years. He was also ordered to pay **restitution** to the phone company and complete 250 hours of community service. His computer was confiscated.

Here, a group of teenage would-be hackers compare notes at the H2K2 Conference in New York City. The three-day conference attracted an estimated 2,000 security professionals and computer activists. Some of the world's best-known hackers unveiled a plan to offer free software to promote anonymous Web surfing in countries where the Internet is censored.

The Article that Changed History

"A magazine article that got me interested in phone **phreaking** long ago... was labeled 'Fiction' in *Esquire* magazine, but it turned out to be real," says Steve Wozniak—founder, along with Steve Jobs, of Apple Computers—on his Web site, www.woz.org. The article, about Cap'n Crunch, started:

> I am in the expensively furnished living room of A1 Gilbertson (his real name has been changed), the creator of the "blue box." Gilbertson is holding one of his shiny black-and-silver "blue boxes" comfortably in the palm of his hand, pointing out the 13 little red push buttons sticking up from the console. He is dancing his fingers over the buttons, tapping out discordant beeping electronic jingles. He is trying to explain to me how his little blue box does nothing less than place the entire telephone system of the world, satellites, cables, and all, at the service of the blue-box operator, free of charge.... You can call yourself from one pay phone all the way around the world to a pay phone next to you. And you get your dime back, too.

Hacker Creates International Incidents

In 2001, Scottish hacker Gary McKinnon was allegedly looking for government coverups of UFOs when he hacked into the U.S. military's computer systems. Using a computer in London, McKinnon spent more than a year cracking computers owned by the Army and NASA. He deleted files, crashed operating systems, copied data, and left notes to the computer's owners suggesting that their security was no good. His work resulted in the Army's work being seriously disrupted just after the attacks of September 11, 2001.

London police caught McKinnon in 2002. After his computers were seized he was indicted by a federal court in Virginia, but remained at liberty while the U.S. and U.K. wrangled the details of his extradition. In 2012 the British government decided that it would not send McKinnon to the U.S. As of 2015, McKinnon's status was still somewhat uncertain; there was some suggestion that if he visited his father in Scotland he might risk extradition. McKinnon has numerous supporters online who welcomed the U.K.'s decision to ignore the United States' extradition request.

In 2012 and 2013 another British man, Lauri Love, hacked into the some of the same U.S. computer systems as well as computers at the U.S. Federal Reserve and the Environmental Protection Agency. The U.S. requested his extradition in 2015, possibly opening up another politicised case over whether the U.S. could demand that the U.K. send it hackers that attack its computer systems.

The Cuckoo's Egg Case

A problem facing law enforcement agencies is finding out where an attack comes from. Is it a foreign intelligence agency, commercial espionage, criminals trying to steal money, or teenage hackers out for the buzz? The government is reluctant to talk about espionage, but there can be no doubt that it happens. In 1989, Clifford Stoll, a systems administrator at the University of California, Berkley, found a discrepancy of just 75 cents in an account. He set about finding the reason, and it led him to a West German gang of hackers. He tells the story in his best-selling book, *The Cuckoo's Egg*. It soon became clear that many military, science, and industry computers in the United States, Western Europe, and Japan had been penetrated. The trail led to West Germany (before reunification) and a gang of hackers. They were stealing passwords, programs, and other information that they sold to the Soviet KGB. Three members of the gang were sentenced to time in prison.

A year after the Cuckoo's Egg case, intrusions into more than 500 military and civilian government computers and private systems were discovered. Operation Solar Sunrise was launched in response. At least 200 unclassified military systems were penetrated, including seven Air Force bases, four Navy installations, and the Department of Energy National Laboratories. A 24-hour guard was placed on all military computers to detect and stop intrusions.

The attacks were happening as the military buildup for the Gulf War was taking place. Links to some Gulf region Internet Service Providers heightened fears that Iraq was behind the attack. A huge interagency investigation was launched. For four days, the U.S. government did not know who was attacking key defense computers essential to deploying forces in the Gulf. The trail led to two high school students in Colverdale, California. They had learned their skills from 20-year-old Ehud Tenebaum, an Israeli hacker known as "The Analyzer," who was passing on his knowledge before retiring. He also had four Israeli pupils.

The Datastream Cowboy and Kuji

In 1994, U.S. agents sat in a bunker and watched as a hacker signed on to a computer using the user name of a high-ranking Pentagon employee. As the "Datastream Cowboy" went through battlefield simulation data, artificial intelligence files, and reports on Gulf War weapons, the agents' fingers flashed across their keyboards in an attempt to identify the hacker. However, they could not even establish in which country he (or she) was sitting.

The elusive Kuji: working with the Datastream Cowboy, he was seen as the number-one threat to U.S. security because he probed secret sites in both America and the Far East. But he was untraceable as he launched attacks from three continents. It took two years to uncover him.

When he left the Pentagon computer, the agents "followed" him and watched, horrified, as he tried to get access to a nuclear facility in Korea. They feared the attack would appear to be coming from a Pentagon computer and that Communist North Korea would see it as an American attack. However, the target was in South Korea. In a few weeks, the Datastream Cowboy had become the number-one threat to U.S. security. He was working with an even more accomplished hacker called Kuji. They were untraceable, going though computers in South Africa, Mexico, and Europe before launching their attacks. In less than four weeks, the Datastream Cowboy and Kuji entered the Rome Laboratory, at the Griffiss Air Base in New York State, 150 times.

The Hackers Are Finally Traced

Eventually, it was old-fashioned police work that identified the Cowboy. An informant who surfed the Net discovered that the Datastream Cowboy's cyberspace hangout was at an ISP in Seattle. The informant chatted with him and before long, found out he lived in England. The Cowboy even gave the informant his phone number.

Scotland Yard's computer crime unit then traced him to a house in a dreary north London suburb. Telephone traces revealed he was dialing Bogota, Colombia, and from there, using a free phone line to hack into the military sites. The Datastream Cowboy was not a dangerous spy, but a 16-year-old music student named Richard Pryce, who had barely scraped through his computer science exam at school.

It was two years before Kuji was discovered. He was Matthew Bevan, a 21-year-old computer worker in an insurance office in Cardiff, Wales, whose bedroom was covered with *X-Files* posters. Pryce later told *The Sunday Times* of London, "It was just fame, a challenge. I was amazed how good I got at it. It escalated very quickly from being able to hack a low- profile computer, like a university, to being able to hack a military system."

Pryce was fined £1,200 (about $2,000) after his lawyer insisted it was an exaggeration when the Senate Armed Services Committee was told that he had caused more damage than the KGB and was the "number one threat to U.S. security." A charge of conspiracy against Pryce and Bevan was dropped, and Bevan walked free.

America's Most Famous Hacker

Kevin Mitnick claims to be America's most famous hacker and was once on the FBI's Most Wanted List. He started out stealing computer manuals from Pacific Bell in Los Angeles and kept going. His grandmother said, "He's got a very curious mind. He's never destroyed anything. He loves technology; he wouldn't hurt it." And his attorney, Donald Randolph, said, "He's a recreational hacker. He didn't do it for economic gain or damage anything, and there's no allegation he attempted to damage anything."

That has not made Mitnick any more popular with the law enforcement agencies. He has been held in the Los Angeles Metropolitan Detention Center, where violent criminals are often held. The U.S. Supreme Court has turned down his appeals for bail twice. Mitnick has been charged and sentenced seven times.

He first gained national notoriety in 1982, when he hacked into the North American Defense Command (NORAD), an escapade said to have inspired the movie *War Games*. However, he was not charged with that. In his early days, he also gained control of telephone offices in New York and California, also without charges following. He first went to jail after hacking into Digital Equipment Corporation computers.

In 1992, subject to a federal arrest warrant, Mitnick became a fugitive.

He went on a hacking spree but was traced by a computer expert who discovered that his home computer had been hacked.

Mitnick was held in custody for three years before a plea bargain in 1999 put him into prison for another year. His case generated enormous interest, with a Free Kevin Mitnick Web site and stickers. Steve Gold, news editor of *Secure Computing,* said: "For all he's done, there are despots and murderers out there who have suffered less than Kevin."

Hero or villain? Kevin Mitnick, America's most famous hacker, was once on the FBI's Most Wanted List. But some people think he fell victim to an overbearing state that got his activities over two decades out of proportion. He is shown here in 1995, the year he was jailed for 14 months.

In the 2010s, Mitnick was a legitimate businessman, running—appropriately enough—a computer security firm called Mitnick Security Consulting, for which he provided security advice to Fortune 500 companies. He has spent the past several years building his reputation as an expert on hacking and security systems and publishing books on his experiences. His adventures were the subject of the 2000 film *Track Down*.

Supporters of Mitnick hacked into the Senate Web page and defaced it. Such action is what is now being called hacktivism. And that is the problem for the authorities in handling hacking. Being on the receiving end of a hack, you do not know at first if it is coming from terrorists, spies, criminal gangs, or teenagers honing their computer s kills.

Kevin Mitnick's Record

1981: Computer fraud; one year probation (California)

1987: Computer fraud; sentence unknown (California)

1989: Hacked into MCI and Digital Equipment computers; one year in low-security prison (partly at a halfway house for people with compulsive disorders) and three years supervised release (California)

1992: Hacked into Department of Motor Vehicles computers; sentence unknown (California)

1995: Possession of unauthorized access devices; eight months in jail (North Carolina)

1995: Violation of supervised release; 14 months in jail (California)

1996 (came to trial 1999): Computer fraud, wire fraud, and possession of unauthorized access devices; held in custody from arrest to trial and sentenced to a further year in jail.

2000: Beginning of Mitnick's new career as a security expert, consultant, public speaker, and author.

Julian Assange, Edward Snowden, and U.S. Security: Criminals or Heroes?

In 2006, Australian programmer Julian Assange founded the website WikiLeaks, on which he published the fruits of his hacking labor. WikiLeaks became famous in 2010 when it published classified documents leaked from U.S. military computers. He published materials from the wars in Afghanistan and Iraq, hundreds of thousands of diplomatic communications, and files from the U.S. military prison in Guantanamo, Cuba. Opinion was divided on Assange's work. The U.S. government took a dim view of his activities, accusing him of violating the Espionage Act and endangering national security. Others praised him for fighting for transparency and civil liberties.

American Edward Snowden was another hacker who cracked the code of U.S. classified documents. In 2013 he leaked a large amount of classified information from National Security Agency computers, revealing that the United States had been spying on a large number of people. Snowden was charged with stealing government property and violating the Espionage Act. He fled to Russia, where he remained as of 2015.

Protesters in Berlin react to Snowden's revelation that the United States was conducting surveillance on German citizens.

No System is Safe

By the 2010s, many people realized that no computer system was completely free from the threat of hackers. In 2013, the department store Target was the victim of a massive hacking attack that stole data from 110 million customers' store credit cards. Actress Jennifer Lawrence had nude photographs stolen and leaked online in 2014. The following year hackers got into the data files of infidelity dating service Ashley Madison and revealed the names of millions of users to the world. Also in 2015, a hacker announced that he could hack into any Apple iCloud account. Apple recommended two-step verification for entering accounts and continued to improve security measures—but it is clear that the hacking game will continue.

Text-Dependent Questions

1. What is hacking?
2. Who was Kevin Mitnick?
3. What is WikiLeaks?

Research Projects

1. Hackers such as Edward Snowden and Julian Assange are alternately considered heroes and villains, depending on who you talk to. What do you think? Are activities like theirs dangerous threats to national security or blows for freedom from an oppressive state?

2. How safe is social media? Find out some things that have gone wrong involving hacking and social media.

3. What possible worst-case scenarios can you envision that involve hacking?

CHAPTER 3

THE THREAT INSIDE

Words to Understand

Embezzle: to appropriate something fraudulently for one's own use

Intrusion detection system (IDS): software designed to detect misuse of a system

"REVENGE IS A KIND OF WILD JUSTICE, WHICH THE MORE MAN'S NATURE RUNS TO, THE MORE OUGHT LAW TO WEED IT OUT," THE ENGLISH ESSAYIST FRANCIS BACON WROTE IN THE 17TH CENTURY. TO TODAY'S POLICE, IT IS A THOROUGHLY MODERN SENTIMENT, AS DISGRUNTLED EMPLOYEES INCREASINGLY USE COMPUTERS TO TAKE REVENGE. A FEW YEARS AGO, SOMEONE WHO FELT HE OR SHE HAD BEEN UNFAIRLY FIRED MIGHT DROP AN IMPORTANT FILE BEHIND A CUPBOARD. NOW, HE OR SHE CAN SET A COMPUTER TIME BOMB IF SKILLED ENOUGH, OR SEND A DAMAGING E-MAIL TO CUSTOMERS IF NOT.

Beware the Disgruntled Employee

Insider computer crime includes both revenge and fraud. Many of these crimes go unreported because companies and government agencies are reluctant to admit that their systems are not as secure as they would like the world to believe. Disgruntled employees have been considered the biggest cyber crime threat, although there are signs that external attacks are overtaking them as access through the Internet increases.

It could be anyone–the most unassuming man or woman in the workplace might be plotting to damage the company. It is often easy to obtain someone else's password and gain entry to an organization's most sensitive data.

High-tech businesses are most vulnerable because many of their employees have the skills needed to hack the system. When the dot-com bubble burst at the start of the millennium and staff were laid off, federal investigators noticed a rise in revenge attacks.

"The whole nature of computer crimes has changed. The problem at big companies is [that] the network administrator is probably the last guy who finds out you got fired, and doesn't cut off your access. Or it's the network administrator who gets fired, and he has access," said Agent Greg Walton of the FBI's San Francisco area computer intrusion squad.

Many employers have set up policies to prevent revenge attacks. When someone is fired, this person is immediately escorted from the building and his or her belongings are sent afterward. The system administrator is informed immediately, and the ex-worker's computer access is stopped. This works as long as the password system is secure, but frequently, people give their passwords to colleagues. It is often the easy and practical way to work. A document is urgently needed, but it is on the computer of someone who has the day off. Rather than come into the office, this person gives the password to a colleague. Others may write their passwords on the bottom of their keyboards. There is a mismatch between the way people interact at work and the needs of computer security.

People who work late and alone in an office are often among the first suspects when an insider crime is detected. Increasingly, security systems are used to record when employees are in sensitive areas of office and factory buildings.

Cyber Crime Facts Circa 2014

The 2014 U.S. State of Cyber Crime Survey, conducted by Pricewaterhouse-Coopers (PwC), the U.S. Secret Service, CSO Magazine, and the CERT Division of the Software Engineering Institute at Carnegie Mellon University analyzed data gathered from over 500 businesses, law enforcement agencies, and government agencies. It evaluated responses for stated threats, concerns, and cybersecurity practices. The results were sobering and suggested that all businesses and governments should be very concerned about the threat of cyber crime. (http://www.pwc.com/us/en/increasing-it-effectiveness/publications/assets/2014-us-state-of-cyber crime.pdf)

77% of respondents to the U.S. State of Cyber Crime Survey had detected a breach of security in the past 12 months.

The average number of reported security incidents in 2013 was 135 per organization.

The average monetary loss was $415,000.

The most common types of cyber crime were network interruptions, denial of service attacks, malware, and phishing.

Financial services experienced a large amount of financial fraud.

Healthcare companies reported large numbers of exposure of private or sensitive information.

72% of reported incidents involved hackers outside the company. Organized criminals were believed to be responsible for only 7% of incidents.

Another small but dangerous portion of hackers are nation-states that might target national systems; unrest in Syria, Iran, and Russia will likely increase this threat.

Hacking by company insiders was more costly than hacking by outsiders.

The larger the business, the greater the threat from internal hackers.

Business partners are a particularly dangerous source of hackers, but few companies have a strategy for evaluating the security of their trusted partners.

The damage is sometimes more embarrassing than anything else. One former contract employee at a technology company hacked the computer and sent e-mails, pretending that these were from management. They told workers the company was going out of business, and the messages also had a pornographic attachment.

Expert Cyber Sabotage

The expert can cause damage that may bring a business to its knees. This is the story of an attack so complex that it took investigators years to discover how it had been done.

Starting the computer server was the first job of the day for the first person to arrive at the manufacturing facility of Omega at Bridgeport, New Jersey. On July 31, 1996, a message stating that a section of the file server was being fixed appeared on the screen. Then the server crashed. The backup tape could not be found. Then it was discovered that the server had not just crashed—more than 1,000 programs needed to make 25,000 products had disappeared. Omega, with headquarters in Stamford, Connecticut, makes high-tech measurement equipment and instrumentation. Before the Omega case was solved, 80 people had lost their jobs, the company had lost $10 million, and growth plans for the company had been derailed.

Suspicion centered on Tim Lloyd, the 37-year-old who, in 11 years with the company, had risen from the machine room to become chief computer network program designer. Tim Lloyd had been fired three weeks before the crash. But if the crash was the result of a crime, how had it been carried out? The Secret Service was called in under a law that makes computer sabotage a federal offense if it causes more than $5,000 damage and affects a computer used in interstate commerce. Special Agent William D. Hoffman started an investigation that would last four years.

The job of finding clues on the hard disk was given to Greg Olson of Ontrack, a data recovery and computer forensics business. "I've never seen this massive a deletion in my 10 years of experience," he said. Eventually, he pieced together odd bits of code and found lines of commands timed to operate on July 31, 1996. Normal deletion code had been modified to replace the normal "deleting" screen message with "fixing." Then, Olson found the same code on one of Tim Lloyd's hard disks.

The jury found Lloyd, who continued to maintain his innocence, guilty of setting up one of the biggest computer "time bombs" ever. He was jailed for 41 months.

"Billion-dollar Bubble"

Large-scale employee fraud has always been a threat to business. Yet, how much of it should be classified as cyber crime? Today, virtually everything that happens in a business involves computers so, inevitably, an employee working a scam on the firm is aided by electronics. This next case dates from the early 1970s, long before the term "cyber crime" had been coined, but it could not have been on the same scale without a computer. That is what makes the "Billion-Dollar Bubble" significant in the history of cyber crime, as well as a spectacular event.

Monitoring of communications networks plays a crucial part in the investigation of computer crimes. If people and transfers of information can be associated, this will often provide the evidence that investigators need before questioning a suspect.

Computer forensics experts employed by the police can often find information that computer users thought they had completely erased when trying to cover their tracks. It is very difficult to conceal the use anyone has made of a computer system.

The Cyber-embezzler

It was old-fashioned police work—putting two bits of information together and seeing a crime—that uncovered a **cyber-embezzler**. A police raid on a bookmaker revealed the unusual betting habits of one man. The man, Roswell Steffen, was a teller who trained new tellers at the Union Dime Savings Bank in New York. Steffen earned a moderate salary, yet placed bets of $30,000 a day. The bank found it difficult to believe, but when bank investigators went through the books, they found Steffan had embezzled $1.4 million. He had a computer terminal with supervisory access and two cash boxes, one containing $10,000 and the other $50,000. He had started by borrowing $5,000 from the cash fund with the intention of repaying from his winnings. When that was exhausted, he borrowed more and had no prospect of repaying it.

For three years, Steffan used a range of tricks to get money. These included reducing deposits made by customers and creating new accounts. Eventually, he was juggling 50 accounts. He made frequent mistakes, yet he was not caught because when auditors found discrepancies he would simply blame them on the inexperience of the tellers he was training and use his supervisory terminal to make corrections

Executives at Equity Funding set up 64,000 fake insurance policies. They then sold these policies to other insurance companies in re-insurance deals. That brought in cash in the first year, but premiums had to be paid to the re-insurance companies in the second year. So more fake policies were created and sold to pay for the premiums. And thus the cycle went on for more than 10 years until the fraud was uncovered in 1973.

By this time, the task of preparing bogus policies was so great that a computer program had been written to generate policies. By the time the whistle was finally blown by an employee who had been fired, 70 percent of Equity Funding's policies were bogus.

Complex Crimes

Accountants Geoffrey Osowski, aged 30, and Wilson Tang, aged 35, worked for Cisco Systems in California. The charges they faced are a sign of the way laws are changing to meet the challenge of new crimes. They were charged with exceeding authorized access to computer systems, computer fraud, and wire fraud. Behind those offenses was the theft of shares worth nearly $8 million.

Osowski and Tang accessed the system used by Cisco to manage stock options and found the control numbers used to track authorized stock-option dispersals. They were then able to create forged forms, which appeared to show they should be issued shares. They set up personal accounts at Merrill Lynch and faxed the forms to the company that was responsible for issuing the shares.

Three times they had shares moved to their personal accounts at Merrill Lynch. In the end, these added up to $7,868,637. When the government seized stock still in the accounts, it raised just over $5 million. An automobile and jewelry were also seized. In addition to 34 months each in prison, the two men agreed to pay restitution.

In 2002, a Computer Security Institute/FBI survey found financial losses from unauthorized insider access ranging from $1,000 to $5 million. The average loss was $275,000. To counter this, there was a move away from reusable passwords, which in practice, are seldom changed. Instead, single-use passwords were combined with cards that identify the user.

How to Make a Strong Password

A good deal of cyber crime occurs because criminals guess user passwords. This is partly because many people still use ridiculously easy passwords, such as "password" or "12345678." Complicated passwords, however, make it hard for users to access their own accounts because they are too easy to forget.

In the 2010s, there was a move away from overly complicated passwords, which are hard for people to remember but can be fairly easy for computers to crack. Instead, security experts recommend that people make up passwords that are easy for them to remember, but not at all obvious to machines.

One way to do this is to make up a sentence, such as "We have two dogs: Ollie and Fluffy." Then take the first letter from each word, plus symbols when possible, and turn that into a password: "Wh2d:O&F." The longer the password, the harder it is for a computer to figure it out, so ideally a password should be at least eight characters.

Cisco Systems in California is a leader in network systems and has developed a range of products to prevent unauthorized intrusions. Their **Intrusion Detection System** watches for changed patterns of behavior as well as using more conventional detection techniques.

The Rise of External Attacks

Rebecca Herold, a computer security consultant, explains that there is a long way to go in improving security. Security people need to be in positions where they have real influence over policy. "I still remember being asked in 1995 why I wanted to be in a 'dead-end' job such as security. The person asking me this told me I could only be spending about four hours a day working on user IDs and access changes. They told me I should look into doing something with a more promising future, because they didn't think security would ever be a position that needed to be filled with the 'technical advances' being made. Okay, this person was an IT manager then, but is now a night-time manager at a convenience store," she says.

While survey results showed that external attacks were overtaking internal attacks, security experts warned about the dangers of complacency and the danger of relying on statistics. Writing in *Information Security Bulletin*, Dr. Eugene Schultz said: "Unfortunately, a lot of the confusion comes from the fact that some people keep quoting a 17-year-old FBI statistic that indicated that 80 percent of all attacks originated from the inside. At the time this statistic was first released, it was almost certainly valid–the computing world at that time consisted to a large degree of mainframes and stand-alone PCs... Today, we have a proliferation of network services (most notably the World Wide Web service) available to the entire Internet community–a truly target-rich environment for would-be attackers."

Dr. Schultz said that while the CSI/FBI survey showed outsider attacks outnumbering internal ones, he believed external attacks were being vastly underestimated. "I'd like to add that any statistics concerning security-related incidents and computer crime are suspect and should not be taken at face value. What is the main point here? Is it that we should ignore the insider threat in favor of the outsider threat? On the contrary. The insider threat remains the greatest single source of risk to organizations. But what I am saying is that it is important to avoid underestimating the external threat."

Text-Dependent Questions

1. What is a revenge attack?
2. Where do most attacks on businesses come from?
3. What is cyber-embezzlement?

Research Projects

1. Have there been any serious attacks on businesses in the past two or three years? What happened?
2. What do banks and financial institutions do to maintain security of their data?
3. How do federal agencies such as the FBI and CIA go about ensuring that their employees do not steal classified information? How often does this happen despite all precautions?

BUSINESS UNDER ATTACK

Words to Understand

Encryption: conversion of data into a secure code

Extort: to obtain something from a person by force, intimidation, or undue or illegal power

Fence (v.): to sell stolen property

Wire-tapping: interception of communications

A NEW KIND OF ROBBER NEEDS A NEW KIND OF COP. MICHAEL MORRIS IS ONE OF THE NEW COPS. BORED WITH HIS $96,000-A-YEAR JOB WITH ACCOUNTANTS PRICE WATERHOUSE (AS IT WAS THEN CALLED), HE PACKED IT IN AND ENROLLED IN THE FBI ACADEMY FOR A $2,000 MONTHLY PAYCHECK. WHEN HE GOT HIS MAN AFTER A FIVE-YEAR INVESTIGATION, HE WAS HAILED AS THE FBI'S LEADING COMPUTER GUMSHOE. THE ROBBER IN THIS HIGH-TECH COPS-AND-ROBBERS STORY WAS CALVIN CANTRELL. A LETTER FROM HIM READ ALOUD IN A DALLAS COURTROOM SAID, "MY PARENTS TAUGHT ME GOOD ETHICS, BUT I HAVE DEPARTED FROM SOME OF THESE, LOST MY WAY SOMETIMES. I WAS 25 AND LIVING AT HOME. NO JOB, AND NO FUTURE. ... ALL I EVER REALLY WANTED WAS TO WORK WITH COMPUTERS." CANTRELL DID WORK WITH COMPUTERS—THOSE OF SOME OF THE LARGEST CORPORATIONS IN THE WORLD, BUT WITHOUT AUTHORIZATION.

Shawn Fanning, founder of Napster, the once-dominant Internet music-swapping service, which found itself under attack from the big music corporations. They saw Napster as aiding pirating, otherwise called intellectual property theft.

Calvin Cantrell and the Phonemasters

Cantrell belonged to a gang the FBI called the Phonemasters. Their high-tech crimes began in a low-tech way with dumpster diving. They collected old phone books and telephone system manuals that had been thrown away and gained enough information to get into phone company systems. They were in the business of selling information. They broke into the networks of AT&T, British Telecom, Southwestern Bell, and Sprint. They got into the Nexis/Lexis databases and Dun and Bradstreet. They hacked into a cache of unpublished phone numbers at the White House and conspired to break into the FBI's National Crime Information Center (NCIC).

The Phonemasters had a price list: personal credit reports, $75; state motor vehicle records, $25; FBI Crime Information Center records, $100. For $500, they would provide the address and phone number of any "celebrity or important person." The customers were private investigators, so-called information brokers, and, through middlemen, the Sicilian Mafia. Information was sold to someone in Canada, who transferred it to someone else in the United States, who sent it to another middleman in Switzerland, who then sold it to the Mafia.

Information is valuable. Businesses and government agencies protect it, but criminals are increasingly turning to the Internet as a way into the vast databases of information that can be sold. Other criminals and unscrupulous corporations may be among the customers.

Michael Morris first heard about the Phonemasters from a Dallas private investigator. He listened to the price list and persuaded the investigator to meet Cantrell while wired for sound. After listening to the tapes, the FBI put in a device that recorded the numbers dialed on Cantrells line. It showed calls to many phone company numbers and two to unlisted numbers at the White House. However, the existing legal powers in 1994 were not enough to investigate this case.

Morris realized that he needed new powers to crack the case, and he was determined to get them. While tapping telephone lines for voice was allowed (with many restrictions), intercepting the impulses generated by computer modems was not. He wrote to the FBI's headquarters in Washington, D.C. and to the federal district court in Dallas. "It was," says Morris, "one of the hardest techniques to get approved, partly because it is so intrusive. The public citizen in me appreciates that. It took a lot of educating federal attorneys."

Developing New Detection Equipment

That was the legal issue. The other issue was getting equipment that would do the job. Morris worked with technicians at the FBI Quantico engineering lab to specify the equipment to convert the modem tones back into digital signals—technically, a difficult task.

Michael Morris took a big pay cut to enroll here at the FBI Academy to learn how to be an agent. He turned out to be no ordinary agent, but rather the man who has been called the FBI's leading computer gumshoe. His five-year investigation is a classic of cyber-crime detection.

While he waited for the equipment, another Phonemasters scam was uncovered. They created fake telephone numbers that forwarded calls to phone-sex lines in Germany. How the Phonemasters got people to call the numbers was never discovered, but Cantrell got a payment of $2,200 from Germany for generating the traffic. The Phonemasters also diverted some FBI field office lines to premium-rate numbers in Germany, Moldavia, and Hong Kong. That prank resulted in the FBI being billed $200,000 for illegal phone calls.

When Morris's $70,000 "magic box" arrived, it was installed in a leaky, unheated warehouse. This site was chosen because it was between Cantrell's home and the nearest telephone exchange. The 10 agents taking turns monitoring the data kept a tarp handy to protect the equipment when it rained. With enough data collected and analyzed, Cantrell and another man, Cory Lindsay, were convicted in 1999. Cantrell was jailed for two years, while Lindsay was sentenced to 41 months. Other members of the gang are still at large. Their activities are said to have added up to $1.85 million in business losses.

The significance of the Phonemasters case is that it introduced the concept of **wire-tapping** for data rather than voice. However, this is much more of a fishing expedition than with a voice intercept, where it is possible to quickly reject and destroy material that is not relevant to an inquiry. Furthermore, technological change often makes intercepts more difficult. Increasingly, even home computers use digital rather than analog modem signals and **encryption**.

Russian Computer Criminals

However, all the information in the world is no help if the cop cannot get the cuffs on the robber. This was the problem for Special Agents Marty Prewett and Michael Schuler. They knew the names of their men and they knew where they lived—in Chelyabinsk in the eastern foothills of Russia's Ural Mountains. Since the fall of Communism, organized crime has flourished in the former Soviet states, and well-educated, computer-literate men with poor prospects of reasonably paid jobs have turned to computer crime. Much of the intrusion into sensitive private and government databases around the world is traced to Russia.

Chelyabinsk in the foothills of the Ural Mountains remains an impoverished city in post-Communist Russia, a seemingly unlikely place to find hackers. But from here emerged two of the most significant cyber criminals to fall into the hands of the FBI.

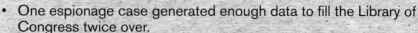

The FBI Investigates

- One espionage case generated enough data to fill the Library of Congress twice over.
- The increased use of encryption for faxes and cell phones, as well as computer communications, has placed a "tremendous burden" on the FBI's electronic surveillance technologies.
- Every increase in the size of computer hard drives increases the work of computer forensic investigators. Even if the disk is not full, every part of it has to be examined.
- Investigation of an **extortion** case required millions of Web sites to be sifted.

Prewett and Schuler were investigating Russian computer intrusions directed at Internet Service Providers, e-commerce sites, and online banks in the United States. The hackers used their unauthorized access to the victims' computers to steal credit card information and other personal financial information. They often tried to extort money from the victims with threats to expose the sensitive data to the public or damage the victims' computers. Stolen credit card numbers were used to generate cash to pay for computer parts purchased from vendors in the United States.

Since the agents could not go to Russia and arrest them, they decided they would have to tempt them to the United States. Accordingly, they created a start-up computer security company named "Invita" in Seattle, Washington. Posing as Invita personnel, the FBI men contacted Vasiliy Gorshkov and another man, Alexey Ivanov, by e-mail and telephone. The Russians agreed to prove their skills by trying to hack into a computer system. They broke into the network without realizing that the FBI had provided it. Having demonstrated their hacking skills, Gorshkov and Ivanov agreed to visit Seattle to talk business.

The Criminals Take the Bait

Unsuspecting, the two arrived in Seattle for their meeting with Invita executives. It seemed to them to be going well—until they were arrested. Gorshkov and Ivanov were charged in the Western District of Washington with conspiracy and 19 additional crimes involving Speakeasy, Nara Bank, Central National Bank, Waco, and PayPal, the Internet payment site. A few days after the two men were arrested, the FBI obtained access via the Internet to two of the men's computers in Russia.

Data copied from the Russian computers provided the investigators with a wealth of evidence of the men's computer hacking and fraud. They had large databases of credit card information that was stolen from Internet Service Providers, like Lightrealm of Kirkland, Washington. Details of more than 56,000 credit cards were found on the two Russian computers. Stolen bank account numbers and other personal financial information regarding customers of online banking at Nara Bank and Central National Bank, Waco, were also found.

The conspirators had gained unauthorized control over numerous computers—including computers of a school district in St. Clair County, Michigan—and then used those compromised computers to commit a massive fraud involving PayPal and the online auction company eBay.

Gorshkov's programs created associated accounts at PayPal with random identities and stolen credit cards. Additional computer programs allowed the conspirators to control and manipulate eBay auctions. They acted as both seller and winning bidder in the same auction and then effectively paid themselves using the stolen credit cards.

The PairGain Hoax

By comparison, the idea behind the PairGain hoax was simplicity itself. People logging on to financial bulletin boards hosted by Yahoo! and others got a tip that a California telecom equipment company was to be taken over. The Israeli buyer was to pay $1.35 billion. There was a link to an apparent news item at Bloomberg, the financial information service. PairGain stock rose by 31% on the NASDAQ Exchange. However, it was a hoax. Thousands of victims who bought shares as a result of the false tip lost large sums when the price collapsed. The perpetrator of the hoax had covered his tracks well, but not well enough to prevent investigators from tracing him through a web of e-mail addresses. The fake Bloomberg page was on a free site that looked like the real thing, and links took visitors to the real Bloomberg site. The person who had set up the fake site registered with a first name of "headlines" and a second name of "99." He also gave a Hotmail e-mail address.

Eventually, analysis of IP addresses—the numbers by which computers are identified—led to Gary Hoke, a PairGain employee in Raleigh, North Carolina. However, he had subsequently gotten "cold feet" and had never actually profited from his scheme.

Internet Auction Fraud

Internet auctions have become among the most frequent scenes of cyber crimes. They range from major frauds, like selling fake pictures and upping the price by putting in "shill bids"—false offers made by an associate to push the price up. In one case, a fake painting was sold for $135,000, but most auction frauds are smaller.

For example, the Internet is a great way for a man to buy his daughter's birthday present if he lives a long way from major stores. Reaching an auction site, he finds a Barbie doll. It looks cute—just the right gift. It does not take long to confirm the purchase and put a money order in the mail. The Barbie doll never arrives, but the money order is cashed.

At the height of the dot-com boom, prices of high-tech companies soared on the Nasdaq Exchange. An elaborate Internet scam sent the price of one company's stock up by 31%, but the hoaxer lost his nerve and did not take a profit.

That is the profile of a typical Internet fraud. Seven out of 10 victims are men and three-quarters of them are between the ages of 20 and 50. Someone living in Alaska is three times more likely to be the victim than someone living in Maryland. The Internet Fraud Complaint Center that compiled these figures found that more than half of all complaints were about auctions and of those, 27% were about the nondelivery of Beanie Babies. Much Internet fraud is old tricks pulled in new ways. Mail-order scams have moved into cyberspace, and thieves have found a new way of disposing of what they have stolen.

Two Michigan men were charged, according to Associated Press (AP), with committing old-fashioned shoplifting with a high-tech twist—**fencing** thousands of dollars in stolen goods through the Internet auction site eBay. Police said the pair shoplifted $40,000 worth of goods from discount stores in Michigan, Ohio, and Indiana, and then sold about half of it on eBay to buyers around the world.

Dennis Moran, a 19-year-old hacker who used the handle "Coolio" in chat rooms, was once thought to be responsible for a series of Denial of Service attacks but eventually pleaded to three misdemeanors. He was sentenced to one year's incarceration and ordered to pay $15,000.

Online Auction Fraud

- According to the Internet Crime Complaint Center (IC3), in 2008 about 25% of all complaints involved online auction fraud.
- Fraud goes in both directions. One of the most common is an overpayment fraud, in which the buyer sends the seller a counterfeit check or money order for more than the purchase price and asks for a refund of the difference.
- High value items can produce wire transfer scams, in which the buyer wires money to the seller, who is never heard from again.
- Most scams are run by individuals, but some are operated by groups from other countries. Romanian and West African organized criminals are common culprits.
- To avoid being a victim, never give out your social security number or driver's license number, be skeptical of super-low prices, and never send a wire transfer if that is the only form of payment the seller accepts.
- If you are the victim of an auction fraud, contact the IC3 or the Federal Trade Commission.

A detective explained their technique: the two men would first buy something like a wheelbarrow that came in a large box. They would then empty the box, return to the store, and fill it with high price items, like digital cameras and radios. They would then pay for the "wheelbarrow" again and walk out of the shop with their loot. They then offered the stolen property on the Internet auction site.

"Don't steal music"

Just when you think you have heard about every possible computer crime, someone invents a new gizmo and someone else applies it to crime. One young man walked into a store, Dallas Comp USA, listening to music on an iPod. He walked up to an Apple Mac and used a FireWire to plug the iPod into the computer, then copied $500 worth of Microsoft software. With the speed of the iPod, the 200 MB of software was transferred in less than a minute.

Music Theft

Pirating of software, music, films, and books and the stealing of trade secrets is called intellectual property rights theft. As long ago as 1997, the American Society of Industrial Security put losses at $2 billion a month. Since then, faster connections have made it easier to download large music files and even films from the mushrooming number of sites. After Napster settled in the courts, the flow of pirated music has slowed only a little. The owners of intellectual property say it is their income and jobs that are threatened. Opponents point out that they do not see the global entertainment and media groups suffering.

The Recording Industry of America suggested that music piracy in the 2000s cost the U.S. economy $12.5 billion each year. Some 30 billion songs were illegally downloaded between 2004 and 2009. The RIAA reported that revenues from digital media hit $4.4 billion in 2013 and accounted for 64 percent of industry revenue, which seems like a lot but is in fact part of declining sales. After Napster appeared in 1999, music sales in the United States had dropped from $14.6 billion that year to $7 billion in 2013.

In cyberspace, where everything is digital information, intellectual property is set to become a hot debate. It is predicted to become an even hotter issue than it was at the height of the Napster case.

Former Apple CEO and cofounder Steve Jobs, who died in 2011, is shown here announcing a new version of the iPod Nano. Jobs was a major player in the push for electronic distribution and enjoyment of music.

Text-Dependent Questions

1. Who were the Phonemasters?
2. Who were the Russian computer criminals?
3. What is encryption?

Research Projects

1. A good deal of cyber crime comes from people living in other countries. Which countries produce the most cyber crime? Why is it so hard to stop them?
2. Now that music and video are widely available for sale, rent, and streaming, how big a problem is piracy in the United States and other countries?
3. Is music piracy really a big problem? Consider both sides of this issue.

VIRUS ATTACK

Words to Understand

Distributed Denial of Service (DDOS) attack: a malware attack that floods all the bandwith of a system or server, causing the system to be unable to service real business

Malware: computer software specifically intended to disrupt the operations of another computer or system, steal information, or do other harmful things

Trojan Horse: a program that pretends to be routine and harmless in order to gain entrance to a computer system, where it turns out to be harmful

Worm: a computer program that enters one computer and replicates itself to spread to other computers; unlike a virus, it does not have to attach itself to other files

COMPUTER VIRUSES HAVE THE MEANS OF INSIDIOUSLY FINDING THEIR WAY INTO OUR COMPUTERS, BEATING DOWN OUR "IMMUNE SYSTEMS," AND DOING THEIR DAMAGE, JUST LIKE THE COMMON COLD VIRUS. THE DIFFERENCE IS THAT COMPUTER VIRUSES ARE MANMADE WITH THE INTENTION OF CAUSING DAMAGE. WHEN ROBERT MORRIS UNLEASHED HIS *WORM* IN 1988, IT BROUGHT HALF THE INTERNET TO A STANDSTILL. THERE WERE NO DEFENSES. THE WORLD WAS NOT EXPECTING IT, AND THERE WAS NO ANTIVIRUS SOFTWARE TO ACT AS THE IMMUNE SYSTEM.

Every computer user is likely to suffer a virus attack at some time. At the least, these are annoying, but some cause real damage, destroying valuable files and software. Sensible computer users use antivirus software and remain aware of potential weaknesses in their systems.

Malware: Worms, Viruses, Trojan Horses

Malware is ubiquitous. The term is short for "malicious software" and it can refer to all manner of insidious programs—viruses, worms, **Trojan horses**, spyware, ransomware, and other fanciful terms for programs that enter unwitting computers and take them over. There are subtle differences between types of malware.

A virus is a program hidden within another program that makes copies of itself and inserts them into other programs, where they do evil things like destroy data and display mocking messages.

A worm is similar to a virus, in that it replicates itself, but it does not need to be attached to another program. Worms might just make multiple copies of themselves, which is annoying, or they might do something worse, such as corrupting or deleting files.

A Trojan horse is a program that appears friendly, causing a user to invite it in—like the Trojan horse in the *Iliad*—and once inside executes malicious code.

Spyware secretly collects information on a person. Adware displays advertisements, which can be quite annoying; it may also collect data on the sites a user visits. Ransomware "kidnaps" a computer system until the user pays some sort of ransom.

Malware is a huge problem. Computer security experts are constantly trying to stay one step ahead of the criminals who want to enter computers for various nefarious purposes.

The Morris Worm

Few people noticed the worm in 1988. The Internet was then restricted largely to universities and the defense and intelligence communities. Robert Morris, then aged 24, was a graduate student at Cornell. He released the Morris Worm accidentally, but said he had been influenced by John Brunner's book *Shockwave Rider*. This is about a gearhead warrior trying to overthrow a network-dependent government by attacking its information arteries.

Morris's first encounter with anything that could be called a computer was when his father brought home one of the Enigma code machines used by the Germans in World War II to encrypt messages before they were sent by radio. The British obtained a machine and analyzed how it worked, which helped them to decode these messages. Morris's father was chief scientist at the National Computer Security Center, part of the National Security Agency (NSA). Like most virus writers, Morris was well educated. The motivation of virus writers has puzzled researchers, who conclude simply, "Most will grow out of it." Morris was brought before a court in one of the first major trials under the Computer

A German Enigma encoding machine, like the one Morris's father brought home from work and showed his son. A captured machine helped the British to decode secret German messages and their success probably shortened World War II.

Fraud and Abuse Act of 1986 and sentenced to three years probation and 400 hours of community service. He was also fined $10,000.

Denial of Service Attacks

As people have become more "streetwise" about avoiding viruses and protection software has become more common, another form of attack has become more prevalent. **Distributed denial of service (DDOS) attacks** crash Web servers or, at best, slow traffic to a crawl. A DDOS attack floods the server with an overwhelming number of requests that need a response. DDOS attacks are more recent than hacking or virus writing and were first investigated in 1999. Many major e-businesses, including Yahoo!, have been attacked, as have government sites. The source and motivation of DDOS attacks remains unclear, as it is difficult to find out who is behind them. In many cases, the attackers use fake IP addresses, which hide the real source of the attack. DDOS attacks are illegal under the U.S. Computer Fraud and Abuse Act.

Over the next years, people simply took it for granted that their computers would be attacked by worms and Trojan horses. Viruses became ubiquitous during the 2000s and 2010s. The Sobig Worm, transmitted through attachments on e-mails, infected millions of Microsoft Windows computers in 2003. It was one of the fastest spreading viruses to date. Over the next decade, viruses, malware, and Trojan horses grew ever more sophisticated. This has generated a side industry of virus-protection software and endless articles on how to remove viruses from computers. Virus protection companies track the latest viruses and often find multiple viruses every month.

The Melissa Virus

In 1999, when the Melissa virus was released into the "wild," there were 100 million Internet users in the United States. Just six days after the Melissa virus was released on March 26, 1999, causing an estimated $80 million worth of damage, 31-year-old David L. Smith was arrested in New Jersey. A serious view was taken of the attack, signaled by the people who lined up to comment. Attorney General Janet

Richard Smith retired from the software company he helped to create and devoted himself to his hobby—Internet security. He has found bugs in e-mail software and Web browsers, and he fingered David L. Smith (no relation), the author of the Melissa virus.

Reno said, "In light of society's increasing dependence on computers, the [Justice] Department will vigorously investigate and prosecute computer crimes that threaten our computer infrastructure."

U.S. Attorney Robert J. Cleary said, "The Melissa virus demonstrated the danger that business, government, and personal computer users everywhere face in our technological society. Far from being a mere nuisance, Melissa infected computers and disabled computer networks throughout North America. There is a segment in society that views the unleashing of computer viruses as a challenge, a game. Far from it, it is a serious crime."

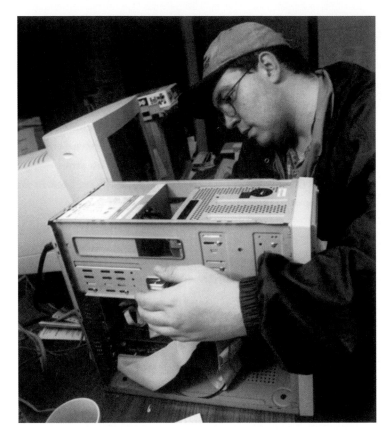

The Chernobyl virus struck hard at New York City Hall. Here, an administrative aide to the mayor is working on one of the virus-hit machines. Normally, repairs after a virus do not involve dismantling a computer.

Viruses and How to Deal with Them

A virus is a program that is loaded onto your computer without your knowledge and runs against your wishes. Viruses can replicate themselves. Even a simple virus is dangerous because it can stop the system by using all available space.

Antivirus software scans incoming files. However, regular updating is necessary to avoid newly developed viruses.

To avoid virus infection, never open e-mail attachments from anyone you do not know. Beware particularly of extensions like .exe. Think twice before opening an attachment on any forwarded e-mail. Viruses can spread readily through networks.

Virus Timeline

1949: Theory of self-replicating programs developed.

1981: First "wild" viruses released; they spread on Apple II computers via pirated games.

1983: Formal definition of a computer virus—a program that can affect other programs by modifying them in such a way as to include a copy of itself.

1986: Two programmers release a virus that infects floppy disks and gives them the volume label "© Brain."

1987: The common virus Jerusalem is unleashed; activated every Friday the 13th, it affects both .exe and .com files and deletes any programs run that day.

1988: Morris Worm is introduced.

1990: Symantec launches Norton AntiVirus, one of the first widely available commercial defenses.

1991: The first polymorphic virus in the wild; polymorphic viruses change their appearance with each new infection.

1992: There are 1,330 known viruses in existence; first media hype predicts Michelangelo virus will crash five million computers; fewer than 10,000 go down.

1993: The first hoax virus warns that opening e-mail will erase the entire hard disk; regular hoaxes ever since.

1999: Melissa virus is introduced, the fastest spreading to date.

2000: The "ILOVEYOU or LOVEBUG" virus is introduced; Stages, the first virus with a false .txt.extension, is introduced, making it easier to lure recipients into opening it.

2001: Kournikova virus succeeds by offering pictures of the tennis star (pictured).

2003: Sobig worm is fastest virus yet seen.

2004: MyDoom virus spreads through email and causes over $38 billion in damages.

2007: Storm Worm, thought to be from Russia, infects nearly 10 million computers running Microsoft systems.

2009: Botnet attacks the United States and South Korea

2012: Flame, an espionage malware that attacked computers running Microsoft Windows, is declared one of the most sophisticated malware programs ever.

2014: The Regin Trojan horse can spread through Web pages and is virtually undetectable by virus detection software.

Onel de Guzman (left), the suspected author of the "ILOVEYOU" virus, never admitted more than that he might have accidentally released it. The Philippines government dropped all charges against him, but it is unlikely he would have been convicted under the law as it then stood.

And New Jersey State Attorney General John Farmer, Jr. said, "Computer criminals may think that they operate in a new frontier without boundaries, where they won't be caught. Obviously, that's not true. We've responded by breaking down traditional borders among federal, state, county, and local law enforcement. In this case, it helped us to make an arrest in less than a week."

The Melissa virus appeared on thousands of e-mail systems disguised as an important message from a colleague or friend. The virus was designed to send an infected e-mail to the first 50 e-mail addresses on the users' mailing lists. It therefore proliferated rapidly. Disrupting computer networks by overloading e-mail servers, it resulted in the shutdown of networks and costly repairs.

David Smith used a stolen America Online (AOL) account and his own account with a local Internet Service Provider to post an infected document on an "alt.sex" Internet newsgroup. The posting contained a message enticing readers to download and open the document in the hope of finding passwords to adult-content Web sites. Opening and downloading the message caused the Melissa virus to infect the victims' computers.

Part of the success of the Melissa virus had to do with the message in the e-mail: "Here is that document you asked for...don't show anyone else;-)."

The "Love Bug" Virus

Two years later, the same technique was used again with the enticing message, "I love you." The so-called "love bug" virus was traced to a 27-year-old man in the Philippines. It had spread around the world in days. The message was irresistible to millions, including people at the Pentagon, CIA headquarters, and Houses of Parliament in London, England.

Sarah Gordon, a researcher at IBM's Thomas J. Watson Research Center, says that most virus writers are intelligent, have good relationships with their parents and other young people, and generally are normal in tests for ethical development. Among the justifications she has found are:

"If my code was used to damage someone's computer, that is the responsibility of the person who's (sic) immature behavior has resulted in damage. Open your mind, and expand your horizons...it's a huge world out there, if you can just get over your fears." And "...this is nauseating...you feel you have the right to censor and condemn the creativity of young, brilliant minds. You fear what you don't understand...."

She says that most young virus writers grow out of it, but she has also identified an older and more technically competent group. She calls them "new-age virus writers" who operate openly and consider virus writing to be

Network Associates in Slough, England, found the cure for the ILOVEYOU virus.

a form of research or self-expression. She doubts if tough legal penalties will work:

> *Those that continue writing and making viruses available to the general public will be seen as "irresponsible" at best, and criminal at worst. That said, it is interesting to note that while some have argued for stronger legal action, research into adolescent at-risk behavior finds that youths are not significantly motivated by fear of legal reprisal or involvement with the criminal justice system. They are more likely to be influenced by peers, family, and significant others whom they like and respect. Fear of the law does not appear to be a major de-motivator for many virus writers, and it appears that for now, the community continues to play itself out over and over again. Until we begin to tackle the root causes of virus-writer motivation, this will continue to be the case; a multidisciplinary approach is required to solve a multifaceted problem. Anything less is oversimplification.*

Text-Dependent Questions

1. What is a virus?
2. What was the Morris Worm?
3. What was the Melissa Virus?

Research Projects

1. Viruses, worms, Trojan horses, and other forms of malware appear every year. What have been some of the worst ones to appear recently?
2. How does malware such as worms and Trojan horses get into computers? How do these programs perpetuate themselves?
3. What does the FBI do to prevent viruses and similar malware from causing serious problems?

LAW ENFORCEMENT AND SECURITY

Words to Understand

Biometrics: use of physical characteristics, such as fingerprints and voice, to identify users

Firewall: software that defends a system from unauthorized use or access

Interpol: an association of national police forces that promotes cooperation and mutual assistance in apprehending international criminals and criminals who flee abroad to avoid justice

NEW TRENDS ARE CONSTANTLY EMERGING IN CYBER CRIME. WHILE IN THE PAST MOST CYBER CRIME WAS COMMITTED BY INDIVIDUALS AND SMALL GROUPS, IN THE 2010S AN INCREASING AMOUNT WAS COMMITTED BY ORGANIZED CRIMINAL GROUPS AND TECHNOLOGY PROFESSIONALS. THE CRIMES ARE THE SAME OLD ONES, THEFT, FRAUD, ILLEGAL GAMBLING, BUT TECHNOLOGY ALLOWS THEM TO EVOLVE TO BECOME MORE WIDESPREAD THAN EVER.

When security really matters, passwords are not enough. Too many people use something obvious, stick the password under a keyboard, or simply give it to a colleague. Here, fingerprint recognition is used to verify the user's identity.

Internet technology and the World Wide Web mean that determined hackers and cyber criminals from anywhere in the world can access highly sensitive information and use it to their advantage.

New Ways to Make Systems Secure

In light of the often-vague threats to businesses and other organizations, computer security has itself become big business. Computer security businesses are growing rapidly, and the consultant arms of the huge international accountancy firms are among the biggest players. Preventing intrusions in the first place is better than the incomplete cure offered by a later police investigation. Just as we protect our homes with locks, burglar alarms, and fire alarms, companies are spending more on securing their computer systems. As with street crime and burglary, there is the fear-of-crime factor. Is the threat overestimated?

Computers are vulnerable because people use them. Passwords are often not secure because they get written down, often on a note stuck inside a desk. Or the password is something simple and easy for another person to guess, like a birthday or the name of a pet. The theory is that passwords should be changed at least every 30 days. However, this can cause irritation and anger, which is often vented on the computer staff by people who find they have been barred from the system. Simply, people have too many PIN numbers and passwords to remember these days and find that they have to write at least some of them down.

The trend now is to augment the password (something you know) with something you have, such as a one-time-use code delivered via text message on a device such as a smartphone. Even if someone gets hold of the password, it is useless without the code. This allows financial companies and banks to implement high levels of security even on home computers. They take the "something you know" idea further by asking personal questions that someone who has stolen a diary with the password written in it will not be able to answer. You might, for example, be asked for a memorable date, your mother's maiden name, or your favorite book.

Card access, like passwords, is far from foolproof. Cards may be lost or stolen. And most people are reluctant to let a security door slam in the face of someone who is following clutching an armful of files.

In Germany, Kim Schmitz was convicted of hacking into corporate computer systems and stealing telephone calling-card numbers. Afterward, he lived a flamboyant lifestyle and claimed to have made millions of dollars from computer security and Internet businesses. He now lives in New Zealand under the name Kim Dotcom, and as of 2016 legal action was pending for copyright infringement associated with his Megaupload file-sharing website, which allegedly cost the entertainment industry $300 million.

Biometrics

To avoid the security problems of human shortcomings, organizations that need to be really secure are moving to **biometrics**. This means identifying some personal characteristic of an individual–fingerprint, voice, keystroke pattern, or the pattern of the retina of the eye. Voice recognition is built into the operating system of Apple Mac computers. The picture shows hand readers, which recognize the characteristics of an individual's hand. They are used to ensure that only authorized people can enter a secure area.

Computer Forensics

Like banks and other traditional businesses, computer-based ventures spend billions on keeping intruders out and trying to stop disgruntled employees from putting their fingers in the till or taking revenge over a perceived injustice.

Police around the world are finding that countering computer crime needs new skills, new laws, and new techniques. Computer forensics—examining computers for traces of how they have been used—is one of the fastest-growing areas of criminal investigation. It has had to spread resources thinly because calls for computer investigations have become routine. In a recent case of a schoolgirl who went missing on her way home from school in England, her computer was examined to see if she had made any contacts over the Internet.

Credit cards should be used with care on the Internet, as they should be anywhere else. The advice is to look for the locked padlock symbol in the browser window that indicates a secure site and to deal only with well-known and reputable companies. If your credit card account displays suspicious activity, contact the card company immediately.

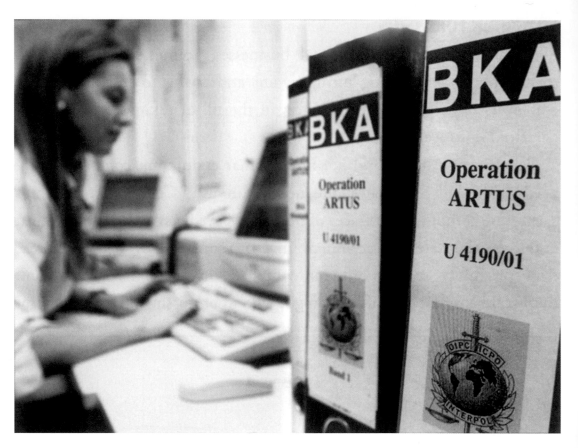

Germany's national police squad, the BKA, uncovered an international pedophile ring. Operation ARTUS, coordinated by **Interpol**, involved police in Canada, Finland, France, Germany, Japan, the Netherlands, Spain, Sweden, Switzerland, the United Kingdom, and the United States.

Hamid Ghodse, president of the International Narcotics Control Board, warned in his 2001 annual report that, "Cyber crime is easy to commit. It requires few resources and can be committed in one country by a person sitting safely in another. It is difficult to fight both the criminals and their crimes in this 'virtual' environment, where national boundaries are irrelevant and personal risk to the criminals and the likelihood of detection are greatly reduced."

Interpol Advice

Interpol has responded to questions it is frequently asked about computer information security by making a number of recommendations. First of all, employers are advised that staff should be aware of (and also accept) the difference between "nice to know" and "need to know" information, meaning that employees should have access only to the information they need to do their jobs effectively.

To secure an Internet connection against hacking, data spying, and data altering, Interpol recommends using a **firewall**. In addition, an Intrusion Detection System (IDS) should be installed to protect against internal attacks.

An Incident Handling System (IHS) should be prepared to minimize damage and losses after an incident. If a company with an IDS realizes a hacker is attacking the system, it is prepared to handle the incident. This will involve disconnecting the system from the Internet and making a full backup so that evidence (for example, IP addresses and log-in times) can be collected. Interpol also recommends notifying the police if there is a serious threat or damage.

Stand-alone computers can be protected through the use of system and screensaver passwords. No one should write passwords under their keyboards, and passwords should be changed frequently. As well as using encryption to protect important and confidential information, Interpol recommends the use of alarm systems.

Viruses should be protected against by using antivirus software. Beware of downloading information that comes from unknown sources and e-mails sent by unknown persons.

Organized crime has adapted to minimize risk. The traditional crime family with a Mafia-style "capo" at its head and a rigid hierarchy is giving way to new structures that are much more difficult to penetrate. These groupings have a fluid network of cells in which national identity is less important than the cell's function and skills. They do not respect national borders, but minimize risks and maximize profits by working across several countries. Investigators can no longer presume that a particular criminal activity falls entirely under their jurisdiction. Like legitimate business, organized crime is going global.

Coordinating the Fight Against Cyber Crime

The United States Department of Justice monitors various types of cyber crime, including hacking, password trafficking, child pornography, SPAM, harassment, and bomb threats. Different agencies handle different types of crime.

Within the U.S., the Federal Bureau of Investigation's Cyber Crime division is dedicated to investigating high-tech crimes, including cyber terrorism. The FBI is constantly gathering information about cyber crime, much of which it reports on its Web site.

The Internet Crime Complaint Center (IC3) is a partnership between the FBI and the National White Collar Crime Center. It provides a platform on which people and businesses can report cyber crime and file official complaints. Complaints are sent to state, local, federal, or international law enforcement divisions, where they are investigated.

The U.S. Secret Service handles cases involving counterfeit currency. It also works with fraud, hacking, and password trafficking.

Police and security agencies, unlike the criminals, are edging slowly toward a more global approach. The biggest step has been the Council of Europe's Convention on Cyber Crime.

The difficulties of coordinating the fight against cyber crime on both sides of the Atlantic are small compared with those in other parts of the world. One survey found that two out of three countries had not updated their laws to deal with cyber crime. Even where they had, the laws were limited in their effect. There is also the problem of different countries cooperating with one another, which has already resulted in the U.K. refusing to extradite hacker Gary McKinnon despite the United States wish that they do so.

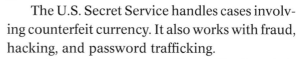

One approach to improving the security of credit card payments over the Internet is to have card readers attached to computers. This overcomes the problem of the theft of card numbers that can be used without the card being physically present.

James B. Cooney was sworn in as the Director of the FBI in September 2013.

Text-Dependent Questions

1. What are the goals of computer security?
2. What are biometrics?
3. What is computer forensics?

Research Projects

1. What is the most current thinking on computer security, including passwords, fingerprint recognition, and so on? What types of passwords are both strong AND easy for users to use?
2. How do computer chips make credit cards more secure?
3. The FBI is particularly interested in stopping criminals who use the Internet for sex crimes such as luring young people into prostitution. What sort of cases have they investigated recently?

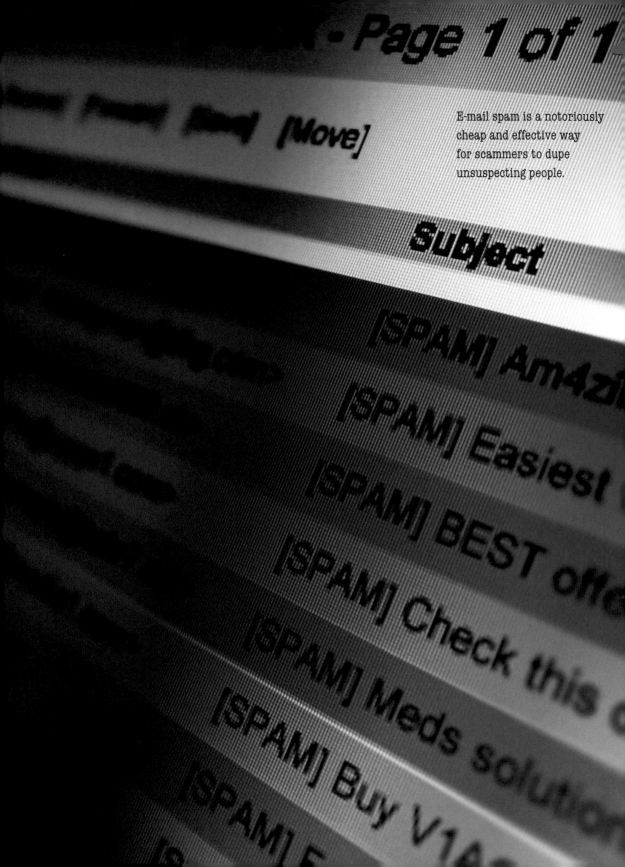

[Move]

E-mail spam is a notoriously cheap and effective way for scammers to dupe unsuspecting people.

Subject

[SPAM] Am4z

[SPAM] Easiest

[SPAM] BEST off

[SPAM] Check this

[SPAM] Meds solut

[SPAM] Buy V1A

SERIES GLOSSARY

Amnesty: pardon given by a country to citizens who have committed crimes

Anarchist: a person who wants to do away with organized society and government

Antiglobalization: against large companies or economies spreading into other nations

Appeal: referral of a case to a higher court for review

Arraignment: a formal court hearing at which the prisoner is asked whether he or she pleads "guilty" or "not guilty" to the charge or charges

Bifurcated: divided into two branches or parts

Bioassay: chemical analysis of biological samples

Biometrics: use of physical characteristics, such as fingerprints and voice, to identify users

Certificate of certiorari: a document that a losing party files with the Supreme Court, asking the Supreme Court to review the decision of a lower court, it includes a list of the parties, a statement of the facts of the case, and arguments as to why the court should grant the writ

Circumstantial evidence: evidence that can contribute to the conviction of an accused person but that is not considered sufficient without eyewitness or forensic evidence

Civil disobedience: refusing, in a peaceful way, to obey a government policy or law

Clemency: an act of leniency or mercy, especially to moderate the severity of punishment due

Commute: to change a penalty to another one less severe

Cryptology: the science and art of making and breaking codes and ciphers

Dactylography: the original name for the taking and analysis of fingerprints

Deputy: a person appointed as a substitute with power to act

Dissident: someone who disagrees with an established religious or political system, organization, or belief

More and more people shop and conduct financial transactions on smartphones, which makes them an attractive target to cyber criminals.

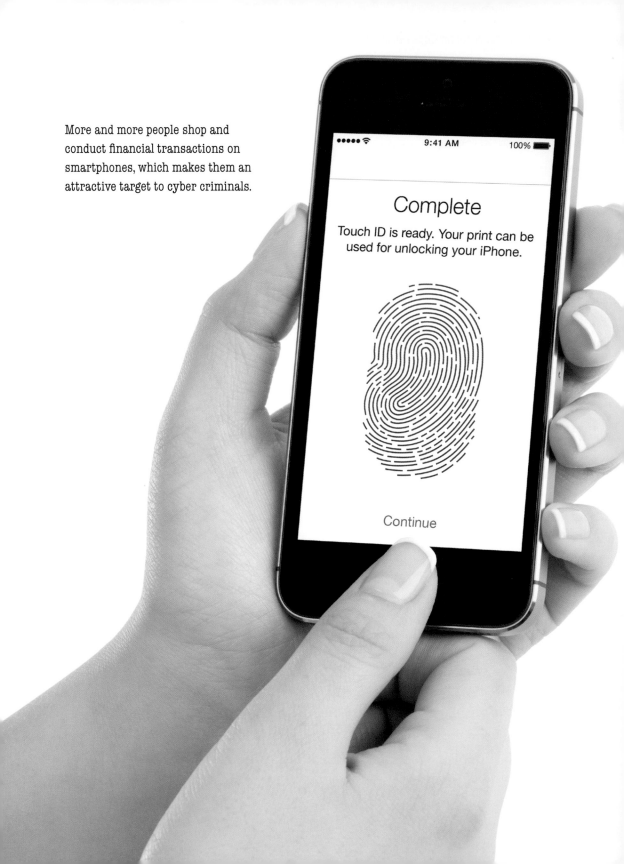

Distributed Denial of Service (DDOS) attack: a malware attack that floods all the bandwidth of a system or server, causing the system to be unable to service real business

Effigy: a model or dummy of someone

Electronic tagging: the attaching of an electronic device to a criminal after he or she has been released, in order to track the person to ensure that he or she does not commit a crime again

Ethics: the discipline dealing with what is good and bad and with moral duty and obligation

Euthanasia: the act of killing or permitting the death of hopelessly sick or injured individuals in a relatively painless way for reasons of mercy

Exhume: to dig up a corpse, usually for examination

Exoneration: a finding that a person is not in fact guilty of the crime for which he or she has been accused

Extortion: the act of obtaining money from a person by force, intimidation, or undue or illegal power

Forensics: the scientific analysis and review of the physical and medical evidence of a crime

Garrote: to strangle someone using a thin wire with handles at either end

Gibbet: an upright post with a projecting arm for hanging the bodies of executed criminals as a warning

Graft: the acquisition of gain (as money) in dishonest or questionable ways

Grievance: a real or imagined wrong, for which there are thought to be reasonable grounds for complaint

Heresy: religious convictions contrary to church dogma and that deviate from orthodox belief

Hulk: a ship used as a prison

Hypostasis: the migration of blood to the lowest parts of a dead body, caused by the effect of gravity

Incendiary: a bomb

Infiltrate: to enter or become established in gradually or unobtrusively, usually for subversive purposes

Intern (v.): to confine or impound, especially during a war

Interpol: an association of national police forces that promotes cooperation and mutual assistance in apprehending international criminals and criminals who flee abroad to avoid justice

Intrusion detection system (IDS): software designed to detect misuse of a system

Junta: a group of military officers who hold power, usually as the result of a coup

Jurisprudence: a system or body of law

Ladder: an early form of the rack in which the victim was tied to a vertical framework and weights were attached to his ankles

Lag: a convict

Latent: present and capable of becoming obvious, or active, even though not currently visible

Lockstep: a mode of marching in step where people move one after another as closely as possible

Lynch: to attack and kill a person, typically by hanging, without involvement of the courts or legal system and often done by a mob

Manifesto: a written statement declaring publicly the intentions, motives, or views of its issuer

Manslaughter: the unlawful killing of a human being without express or implied intent

Martyrdom: the suffering of death on account of adherence to a cause and especially to one's religious faith

Mercenary: a man or woman who is paid by a foreign government or organization to fight in its service

Miscreant: one who behaves criminally or viciously

Molotov cocktail: an explosive weapon; each "cocktail" is a bottle filled with gasoline and wrapped in a rag or plugged with a wick, then ignited and thrown

Money laundering: to transfer illegally obtained money through an outside party to conceal the true source

Mule: a person who smuggles drugs inside his or her body

Mutinous: to resist lawful authority

Paramilitary: of, relating to, being, or characteristic of a force formed on a military pattern, especially as a potential auxiliary military force

Pathologist: a physician who specializes in examining tissue samples and fluids to diagnose diseases

PCR: polymerase chain reaction, a technique of making multiple copies of a small section of DNA so that it can be analyzed and identified

Personal alarm: a small electronic device that a person can carry and activate if he or she feels threatened

Phreaker: a person who hacks telephone systems

Pillory: a device formerly used for publicly punishing offenders consisting of a wooden frame with holes in which the head and hands can be locked

Political asylum: permitting foreigners to settle in your country to escape danger in another country, usually his or her native land

Postmortem: an autopsy; an examination of a dead body, looking for causes of death

Precedent: something done or said that serves as an example or rule to authorize or justify a subsequent act of similar kind

Pyramid scheme: an investment swindle in which some early investors are paid off with money put up by later ones in order to encourage more and bigger risks; also called a Ponzi scheme

Quick: the living flesh beneath the fingernails

Racketeering: the act of conducting a fraudulent scheme or activity

Ratchet: a mechanism consisting of a "pawl," a hinged catch that slips into sloping teeth of a cogwheel, so that it can be turned only in one direction

Repatriation: returning a person to his or her country of origin

Ruse: a subterfuge in order to distract someone's attention

Screw: slang term for a prison guard

Scuttle: to cut a hole through the bottom, deck, or side of a ship

Seditious: of, relating to, or tending toward an incitement of resistance to or insurrection against lawful authority

Serology: the laboratory analysis of blood serum, particularly in the detection of blood groups and antibodies

Siege (n.): a standoff situation, in which a group holds a position by force and refuses to surrender

Slander: a false and defamatory oral statement about a person

Smash and grab: a term used to describe a method of stealing, where thieves break windows (for example, on a shop front or a car) to grab the goods within before fleeing

Statute: a law enacted by the legislative branch of a government

Statutory: authorized by the statute that defines the law

Subversive: characterized by systematic attempts to overthrow or undermine a government or political system by persons working secretly from within

Succinylcholine: a synthetic drug that paralyzes muscle fiber

Vendetta: an often-prolonged series of retaliatory, vengeful, or hostile acts or exchange of such acts

White-collar crime: crime committed by office staff, usually involving theft from the company they work for

Worm: a computer program that enters one computer and replicates itself to spread to other computers; unlike a virus, it does not have to attach itself to other files

Xenophobic: having an unreasonable fear of what is foreign and especially of people of foreign origin

Cloud computing
servers can hold all the
details of our lives.

CHRONOLOGY

1970:	Arpanet, a military research network, is founded.
1971:	First e-mail program is used on Arpanet.
1972:	John Draper (Cap'n Crunch) finds that a toy whistle in a cereal box gives free access to telephone networks; "phreaking" becomes a craze.
1980:	Arpanet crashes because of the accidental distribution of a virus.
1983:	Internet is founded, with the Arpanet split into military and civilian sections.
1984:	The word "cyberspace" is coined by William Gibson in his novel *Neuromancer*.
1986:	"Cuckoo's Egg" Internet espionage case uncovered; Robert Morris's worm is unleashed in the "wild"; it causes a large part of the still-small Internet to crash.
1989:	Kevin Mitnick is convicted of stealing software and codes for long-distance phone lines; Tim Berners-Lee at the Cern high-energy physics lab in Geneva develops an early stage of what will become the World Wide Web; the first Computer Emergency Response Team (CERT) is formed because of concerns following the Morris worm.
1991:	Tim Berners-Lee publishes computer code for the World Wide Web; Kevin Poulsen, Ronald Austin, and Justin Paterson are charged with gaining control of a radio station's phone lines to win major prizes.
1994:	The Datastream Cowboy, Richard Price, described as the greatest threat to U.S. security, turns out to be a 16-year-old music student in London; hackers, directed from Russia, break into Citibank computers and transfer more than $10 million from accounts; all but $400,000 is recovered; Kevin Mitnick is arrested for a second time and charged with stealing credit card numbers; U.S. Defense Department computers are attacked 250,000 times.

1999: Melissa virus causes havoc worldwide; its writer, David L. Smith, is arrested in New Jersey within days; a fake Bloomberg news page is created as part of a scheme to boost the shares of a telecom equipment company, PairGain; Amazon and Yahoo! are almost overwhelmed by denial of service attacks; ILOVEYOU becomes the most famous virus to date; French court rules that Yahoo! must block French users from accessing Nazi memorabilia on its auction site; Napster suspends its service because of litigation over intellectual property rights, and later comes back as a subscription service.

2003: Sobig worm is fastest virus yet seen.

2007: Apple introduces the iPhone, the first Internet-capable smartphone.

2009: Botnet attacks on the United States and South Korea

2010: WikiLeaks publishes confidential U.S. military and diplomatic documents.

2013: Edward Snowden hacks NSA computers, publishes documents on U.S. surveillance activities.

2015: Infidelity website Ashley Madison hacked, millions of users identities spread over Internet. Apple Watch hits the market, allowing people to wear computers on their wrists.

FURTHER INFORMATION

Useful Web Sites

U.S. Department of Justice: www.justice.gov

Federal Bureau of Investigation (FBI): www.fbi.gov

Interpol: www.interpol.int

Council of Europe : www.coe.int

American Civil Liberties Union: www.aclu.org

Internet Crime Complaint Center (IC3): www.ic3.gov

Further Reading

Goodman, Marc. *Future Crimes: Everything Is Connected, Everyone Is Vulnerable, and What We Can Do About It.* Doubleday, 2015.

Holt, Thomas, et al. *Cyber Crime and Digital Forensics.* Routledge, 2015.

Moore, Robert. *Cyber Crime: Investigating High-Technology Computer Crime.* Routledge, 2014.

Schneier, Bruce. *Data and Goliath: The Hidden Battles to Collect Your Data and Control Your World.* W.W. Norton, 2015.

About the Author

Andrew Grant-Adamson is a journalist who became interested in computers when working as an industrial reporter and in 1976 taught himself to use a Commodore Pet, one of the first "personal" computers. He now lives in the English countryside and teaches new media journalism at City University, London.

Only click on links and download attachments from trusted sources.

Protect yourself from cyber frau
by changing passwords often an
avoiding the obvious ones.

INDEX

antivirus software 61, 66–67, 79

Apple Computers 28, 67, 76, 91

Arpanet 23, 90

Berners-Lee, Tim 15, 90

Bevan, Matthew 31

Beyond Hope Convention 26

"Billion Dollar Bubble" 40, 42

biometrics 73, 76, 83

businesses 18, 25, 38–39, 48, 64, 75–76, 80
  external threat 37, 44–45
  information theft from 19, 80
  insider threat 18

Cantrell, Calvin 47–50

Chelyabinsk 50–53

Chernobyl virus 66

Cisco Systems 43

Cleary, Robert J. 65

Cray, Seymour 24

credit cards 12, 14, 18–19, 26, 34, 52–53, 77, 80, 90

Cuckoo's Egg 29–30

Cyber Crime Convention 17, 20, 80

databases 26, 48, 50, 53

Datastream Cowboy 30–31, 90

DDOS (distributed denial of service) attacks 18, 61, 64, 85

death penalty 15

Department of Defense 18, 90

Draper, John 25, 90

Dumpster diving 26, 48

eBay 53, 55

embezzlement 37, 42,

employees 18, 37–38, 40, 42, 53, 79
  dismissed 42
  fraud by 37–38, 40

Enigma machine 62–63

Equity Funding 42

espionage 18, 29, 33, 52, 68, 90

extortion 19, 47, 52, 85

Fanning, Shawn 47

Farmer, John, Jr. 69

Federal Bureau of Investigation (FBI) 7, 16–19, 26, 31–32, 38, 43, 45, 47–50, 52–53, 80–81, 93

fingerprint recognition 6, 72, 76

firewall 73, 79

forensics 40–41, 76, 85

fraud 12, 14, 17–20, 26, 33, 37, 39–40, 42, 53–56, 64, 73, 80, 87

Free Software Foundation 24

Freeh, Louis J. 17

gambling 14, 73

Ghodse, Hamid 78

Gorshkov, Vasiliy 52–53

Gray, Raphael 19

Guzman, Onel de 68

hackers 7, 18, 23–29, 31, 34, 39, 51–52, 74, 90

hacktivism 18, 32

Herold, Rebecca 44–45

Hoffman, William D. 40

identity theft 12, 19, 26

information warfare 18

insider threat 18, 37–38, 45

insurance fraud 42–43

intellectual property theft 47, 56–57

Internet 7, 11–12, 14–19, 23, 26–27, 29, 37, 45, 47–48, 52–56, 61–62, 64–65, 69, 74, 77, 79–80, 90–91, 93

auctions 15, 53–56
  traffic on 15, 64

Internet Service Provider (ISP) 11, 17, 29, 31, 52–53, 69

Interpol 7, 73, 78, 86, 93

Ivanov, Alexey 52

Jobs, Steve 28, 58

Johnston, Michael T. 26

juveniles 26–27

Kelly, Raymond 17

Kournikova virus 67

Kuji 30–31

law enforcement 6–7, 12, 16–17, 26, 29, 31, 39, 73–81

Lindsay, Cory 50

Lloyd, Tim 40

loop-carrier systems 26

Love Bug 67–69

Mafia 48, 79

Massachusetts Institute of Technology (MIT) 23, 24, 26

Melissa virus 64–65, 67, 69, 90

Michelangelo virus 67

Mitnick, Kevin 31–33, 90

modems 49–50

money laundering 14, 86

Moran, Dennis 55

Morris, Michael 47, 49–50

Morris, Robert 61–63, 90

Morris Worm 61 63, 67, 90

music, theft of 47, 57

Napster 47, 57, 91

National Computer Security Center 62

National Security Agency (NSA) 33, 62, 91

online auctions 15, 53–56

Operation Solar Sunrise 29

organized crime 39, 50, 56, 79

Osowski, Geoffrey 43

Packham, Bob 16

PairGain 53, 91

passwords 23, 29, 38, 43, 69, 73, 75, 79, 81

PayPal 52

pedophiles 16, 78

Phonemasters 48–50

pirating 20, 47, 57, 67

policing cyber space 15

pornography 16–18, 20, 80

Prewett, Marty 50, 52

Pryce, Richard 31

Reno, Janet 64–65

revenge attacks 37–38

sabotage 39–40

Schmitz, Kim 75

Schuler, Michael 50, 52

Schultz, Dr. Eugene 45

security 6–7, 20, 23, 26–28, 30–34, 38–39, 43–45, 52, 56–57, 62, 65, 73, 75–76, 79–80, 90

sensitive intrusions 18, 52, 74

shoplifting 55

Smith, David L. 64, 69, 91

Smith, Richard 65

Stallman, Richard 24

Steffen, Roswell 42

Stern, Donald K. 26–27

Stoll, Clifford 29

Tang, Wilson 43

telephone systems 23, 27–28, 48, 87

telephone tapping 48–49

Tenebaum, Ehud 29 30

terrorists 15, 18, 32

theft 12, 19, 26, 43, 47, 57, 73, 80, 88
  information 12, 18–19, 26
  intellectual property 47, 56–57
  music 47, 57

Thompson, Ken 24

Unix 24

viruses 18, 61–62, 64–67, 70, 79
  dealing with 66–67

voice recognition 73, 76

Walton, Greg 38

War Games 25, 32

wire tapping 47, 50

World Wide Web 11, 15, 17, 45, 74, 90

Wozniak, Steve 25, 28

PICTURE CREDITS